"I wanted my letter in the book because I want the council and people who care for kids to know the truth."

— Chardonnay

"Having Camila write to me in that way was a truly amazing experience. There are no words to describe the feelings that my letter provoked. My chapter brought about a profound sense of closure."

— Daisy

"Camila's work with children who have suffered abuse, trauma and emotional deprivation is outstanding. To hear her reflect on their experience is always to have mind and heart expanded, and it is wonderful that we now have such reflection available in this book for a wider public – so that the urgency of what she is talking about just might at last make an impact on the public and on government."

— Dr Rowan Williams, Archbishop of Canterbury

"Camila Batmanghelidjh is a remarkable woman, a child who grew up to fight for children and childhood. This is a truly remarkable book... Read it and resolve that we must do better. If it was hard to write and at times hard to read, imagine what it was to live."

— Shami Chakrabarti, Director of Liberty (the National Council for Civil Liberties)

"Camila Batmangheldjh...tear[s] back the curtains to expose the harrowing stories of some of the "worst" of today's youth. She knows better than most who these young people are: as the founder of two charities, the Place 2 Be and Kids Company, she has devoted much of her life and formidable energies to working with the young cast-offs whom no one else wants to go near... Batmanghelidjh attempts to explain the vulnerability and defensiveness of these young people by revealing what lies behind their impenetrable, frightening masks."

— TES Book of the Week

"Camila Batmanghelidjh has a rare gift for helping the reader to feel empathy with the challenging behaviours and complex survival strategies that very traumatised children often develop... This book must be read by everyone – social workers, therapists, teachers, policy makers and all who touch the lives of children who have been shattered by fear, humiliation and rejection."

— Richard Bowlby

"At heart the book gives Daisy and Chardonnay, Rocky and Mr Mason a voice to articulate the ways they have been failed – and how ways may be found to transform that failure... [T]hough necessarily our attention is held by the stories, our feelings transformed by them, what most impressed me is Camila's ability to offer lucid recommendations for social and therapeutic practice. Care can only be as valuable as the intelligence as well as the compassion that informs it; and, this book compellingly offers both. It should be read by everyone who cares…"

– Network Review – The Journal of the Scientific and Medical Network

"It's so clear, it hurts."

– Ruby Wax

"I would strongly recommend this book to all who are committed to and passionate about giving our children the best possible chance, whatever their professional background."

– Journal of Interprofessional Care, October 2006

"The accounts are deeply moving, sensitive, and perceptive as only one who has spent twenty years working with children across the social divide and has undertaken very extensive training and therapy herself could be."

– British Journal of Psychodrama and Sociodrama (BPA)

"Batmanghelidjh writes with passion and outrage at the extent of the suffering and abuse the child has dealt with, and her letters are filled with empathy, admiration and understanding."

– Children and Society, Vol.21, 2007

"The strength of *Shattered Lives* lies in Batmanghelidjh's passionate conviction that these children have been unjustly treated, but can be reached through the redeeming powers of understanding and love."

– Therapy Today

"Batmanghelidjh offers the reader an alternative view to the one peddled by sections of our media and policy makers, with its superficial understanding of the ills of our society. *Shattered Lives* is about a conviction and passion for children and young people subjected to the worst forms of suffering and an attempt to set their record straight. It both challenges and charges us as individuals and as a society with the collective responsibility of failing to protect and nurture these children. I can honestly say that reading *Shattered Lives* was an experience as opposed to an intellectual exercise – sometimes harrowing, yet not devoid of solutions… It is a clarion call to challenge the malaise in policy and practice and to do better for our children."

– Children Now

"Unusual and compelling…"

– Magistrate

"Deeply moving in every way, this book demands more than our tears."

– 0-19 Magazine website

Shattered Lives

The author has waived any personal financial benefit from this book. All royalties are paid to Kids Company.

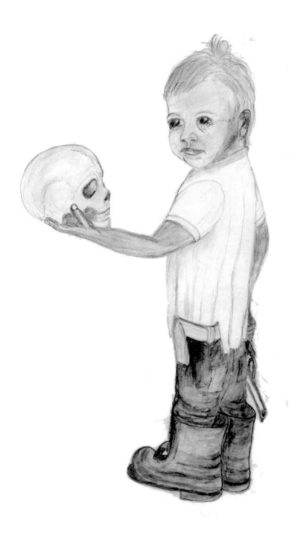

My Childhood by Mr Mason

Shattered Lives

Children Who Live with Courage and Dignity

Camila Batmanghelidjh

Jessica Kingsley *Publishers*
London and Philadelphia

First published in hardback in 2006
Paperback edition first published in 2007
by Jessica Kingsley Publishers
73 Collier Street
London N1 9BE, UK
and
400 Market Street, Suite 400
Philadelphia, PA 19106, USA

www.jkp.com

Library of Congress Cataloging in Publication Data

Batmanghelidjh, Camila.
  Shattered lives : children who live with courage and dignity / Camila
Batmanghelidjh.— 1st American pbk. ed.
    p. cm.
Originally published: 2006.
Includes bibliographical references.
ISBN-13: 978-1-84310-603-6 (pb : alk. paper) 1. Abused children. I. Title.
RJ375.B28 2007
362.76—dc22
                              2007028353

British Library Cataloguing in Publication Data
A CIP catalogue record for this book is available from the British Library

ISBN 978 1 84310 603 6
eISBN 978 1 84642 254 6

Printed and bound in Great Britain

Dedicated to all children, now and then,
and to my mother for letting me be free

Author's note

I am a psychotherapist with more than twenty years' experience of working with children across the social divide. I have founded two children's charities: The Place2Be (www.theplace2be.org.uk), and Kids Company (www.kidsco.org.uk).

Every day of my working life I have come across children whose courage and dignity is breathtaking. This book is dedicated to them.

Many children are loved and cherished but too many are abused, sometimes unwittingly, by parents, teachers, clinicians and politicians, and then blamed. I want to apologize for the distortion.

The child is innocent of the crime. In making the truth visible, I hope we can all learn how not to hurt children again.

Contents

Thank You

I have been deeply touched by the kindness and compassion of complete strangers. Those who have donated money to the charities I founded, and who became partners in caring for vulnerable children. I have met some extraordinary people – businessmen and -women, politicians, clinicians and unemployed people – who all shared their money and wisdom to help our team to develop a special service for children. Sometimes people who were dying requested that money be donated to Kids Company instead of flowers being sent to their funeral.

The trustees of Kids Company, especially Alan Yentob, Peter Wheeler, Richard Handover and Geoff Grant, are owed special gratitude for their courage and tenacity and for not giving up when the going got tough.

Thanks are due to HRH The Prince of Wales for his commitment to young people and for helping to galvanize the business community to assist disadvantaged children. They consider him a true friend.

Cherie Booth QC showed deep compassion and humanity to our most emotionally damaged youngsters.

I worked with morally courageous individuals at Kids Company and The Place2Be. Without the dedication of these staff teams, we would not have been able to reach vulnerable children. I am especially grateful to Tony Cavolli for all his tenacity and wisdom and for being such fun to work with. Karen Stenning is very much loved too for her hard work and ability to chit-chat when mine ran out of steam.

In the writing of this book I was assisted by the administrative team at Kids Company, some of the most inspirational colleagues I have had the privilege of working with. I am especially indebted to all who typed this manuscript from my dictations, Sarah-Jane Fenton, Elizabeth Rodgers, Anthony Traynor, Hanna Heikkilä, and David Van Eeghen, who talked me through the structure of the brain. Daniel Baltzer was a sounding board and a constant source of encouragement, for which I am deeply appreciative. From Dr Carolyn Gaskell and her colleagues I learnt a great deal too.

From the bottom of my heart, I wish to express gratitude to my analyst for helping me understand, and my brothers for accepting their sister as an eccentric! Sadly I don't have a cat to thank, so the final and most special gratitude goes to Jessica Kingsley for helping me dare!

Introduction

I HAVE A clear memory of being a child, what it felt like, what my thoughts were. Everyone has an individual talent. Mine is never having forgotten the feeling of being a child. As an adult I have been a witness to how children are treated by adults. I have seen the love of parents who nurture and protect their children, honouring their childhood. I have also, sadly, seen childhoods devastated by parents who abuse their children, and who neglect them by avoiding the task of parenting. As children grow up with damage, so they damage others, including eventually their own children.

As a society we accept the reality of parental failure. We create structures to protect and treat children who experience extreme failures in loving care. So imagine my horror as I stand by and see these very structures sometimes re-traumatize vulnerable children through their failure to care. I feel indignant and angry as vulnerable children are demonized and blamed, when it is adults who fail to honour the responsibilities of individual and corporate parenting.

I watch clinicians who are dedicated, but also those who engage in deceit. They know where their care structures are failing children, but they do not feel able to speak. Grown and educated men and women become infantile, place their sense of power in managers and politicians. Every day they read the newspapers, and listen to the news as yet another child is demonized. Children are blamed, given anti-social behaviour orders, locked up, paying the price for adult incompetencies. No one speaks up, mindful of their career ladders, their political backs, the peer-pressure. Some disguise their protests so efficiently, so as not to offend – but their neutrality is offensive.

Often the press attempt to tell the story of these children's lives but at times professionals and the press collude in a form of self-delusion, believing the public unworthy of the complex arguments that comprise any explanation of what the children have been through. As a result, fairytale stories are told, which are full of simplistic redemptions or demonic devastations, and basically deliver a diet of platitudes. I watch as childhood is dying. Children cannot afford to be little. The violence in their homes and on the streets could kill them. Being a child to them seems like an insult, a failure of power. It's a burden; childhood is just a waiting room for adulthood. Children are forced to be sexual objects in adults' fantasy and in their reality. Shops sell thongs for six-year-olds, and the predators wait round every corner. Some are violent and some sinister, like the politicians who stand smiling with angelic-looking children as they sign off the latest playground to fat-cat developers.

Political rhetoric expounds doctrines about "respect", but forgets that the respect is in its very essence reciprocal. Give respect, and you shall be given it. The respect politicians peddle isn't far from the tactics of the playground bully – do what I tell you, because I want it. I, the adult, want your respect for my quality of life because I have power over you, the child.

The sexual abuser has power. The teacher who excludes but doesn't protect has power. The social work manager who tries everything not to take the case on has power. I watch the abuse of power by all those who are there to protect children against harm. The social work manager who refuses to take a child without a home into care, leaving her languishing in the police station. Even the police officer was begging. Children who are arrested tell stories of being dumped in vans and driven around so that in the back, the officers could batter them before they got to their destination. Schools, desperate to attain the legitimacy conferred by league table results, ask children with specific learning difficulties to leave before GCSE exams take place. Head teachers send their disturbed children away on trips so that the Ofsted schools inspector will not come into contact with them. There are mental health professionals who will not treat a child because they know the child will eventually commit a crime and end up on the youth offending register, saving them the expense.

I wrote to the directors of social services about children who were prostituting, or who were violent. I begged for their protection, and then social services would write back denying the events as I described them. Imagine being told a teenager with a drug habit of £150 to £170 a day didn't have enough pocket money from social services to buy drugs and therefore she couldn't be addicted. I gasped with shock at receiving this response, wondering if the manager had heard of robberies and the sex trade. I saw stab wounds on little limbs as drug dealers punished the children for unpaid debts or errors in couriering goods. With large companies advertising expensive clothing to youngsters without enough money to buy food, I wondered where humanity had lost its way.

I sat in church for the funerals of children who had no relatives. The priest had to put the choir where the congregation would have been to hide the shame and the truth. Children who were too alone on the streets, who were prey to the perverse, who had been murdered or committed suicide. There was no one to carry the coffin or fill the hole with earth at the graveside, apart from other similarly desolate children, who looked bleak. It could have been any of them in that coffin. The knowing hurt.

This is your modern Western society, where rich street houses implode with wealth. The city erects electronic barriers around its wealth, keeping the poor out and themselves imprisoned. Each night the five star hotels host the latest feast of self-congratulation. The vacuous parties of the rich who gloat, bloated with denial. That very night, the same night that the white tablecloth bears fruits, some child's bed-sheet bears blood. Vigilant children, frozen with terror, store up the insults, and then, when they are strong enough, they deliver them back, fuelled by hate. Powerful in their self-disgust, they are ready to die in revenge.

The urban child warrior, like the religious terrorist, is a new brand of soldier. Their will to die comes from the same space. They have nothing to live for, they are exhausted with living, feelingless, numb and emotionally cold. The urban child soldier, the terrorist, the child who kills, they are all the same children of murdered childhoods.

Time for the truth, for an apology. This book will make you angry, and maybe you will cry at your own lost childhood, or the loss of these children. An apology to these children, and all those other children who deserve one, is the first step in reclaiming our capacity to care. Those of you who did not know the truth about these youngsters' lives – here it is to be witnessed.

Each story is the product of some courageous child who has given me permission to write it. I have only changed the children's names, every other line is as it happened. After I had written it, I read each child's letter to that child, apologizing on our behalf – I apologized for all of us, clinicians, politicians, failed carers, and those whose only crime was ignorance.

None of us can live believing that society is the sum of one individual's capacity to meet his or her own needs. Somewhere, your selfishness would suffocate you, it would take from you your struggle to hold onto your humanity for yourself. We are not alone. To pretend self-sufficiency is to deny a fundamental truth. Human beings can only affirm their living by giving to others. We are reciprocal creatures. We need attachment. We need to be reflected back through the faces of others. Love is the most important experience of our lives. It begins with childhood, it transfers to parenthood and it ends somewhere beyond our comprehension. Love is intrinsic. No amount of money can buy it. The rich without love are shriveled, and the poor struggling with survival cannot be denied it. We are hurting our children by not offering them loving care. We are lying about our failure to protect them.

The murder of childhood is killing us all.

CHAPTER 1

The Witnessing

THROUGHOUT MY LIFE I have worked with vulnerable children. It began when I was nine years old. I used to look after between seventy and ninety children in a nursery in Iran for an hour and a half, while their teachers went to lunch. Looking back, I now realize I had an exceptional gift. But then, my intensive interest in childhood and children seemed normal. I asked my mother to become a member of the Child Development Association, as they would not accept membership from children. The association produced a child development journal; it used to come every Wednesday and I would climb into bed, trying to read it. There was so much I didn't understand, yet I seemed to have been born with a profound knowing.

By the age of fourteen, while at boarding school in England, I had written the model for Kids Company's Arches day centre. I knew that one day this plan would be realized. As children, my brothers used to tease me about my vocation, calling me "Mother Teresa" was intended to be a humorous insult. Yet my younger brother has helped me all the way, knowing I am only living out my destiny. During school holidays I worked in nurseries and by seventeen, I had met a fantastic group of children living in wealthy houses of Kensington, Chelsea and Knightsbridge. They taught me much of what I have learnt.

In material terms, these children were looked after, but they too had intrusions into and interferences with their natural development. They were hothouse children, cajoled to compete for the next private school placement, driven by the need to learn Latin verbs, and their mother's status anxiety.

I remember mothers who had barely left behind their teenage years, who married older men in the hope that money would buy them emotional satisfaction. Their children cut up their Persian carpets and smeared faeces on their fabric wallpaper. Little boys who were fed up of being driven too hard would walk off the bus into the middle of the road, mindless, with no sense of their own identity to preserve.

I also saw manipulative mothers who would sit on the toilet seat pretending to miscarry their baby when they knew they were not pregnant. I watched perfectly manicured birthday parties, where the child was not smiling. In these houses the domestic workers unleashed their rage onto the toddlers; each person seemed consumed by confused desires to be elevated above the rest.

The abuse of children in these houses did not involve knives and guns. Some of the children were battered with belts, locked up – and no one would have guessed, because they went to private school and wore perfectly tailored blazers and velvet dresses with frills. The shine on their little shoes reflected back their sorry faces.

At age nineteen I ran an art club where these rich children would pay for the attendance of ones from an economically disadvantaged background. Every Saturday we covered a building with tarpaulin from top to bottom, all three floors of it. The children would come to be children again. Princes and princesses with fur coats, driven by their security men to the venue, would mix with the youngsters from the local housing estate. The hours passed in magical excitement. We gave them overalls and we let them paint and play; their delight was an experience of childhood that children are often denied.

After completing my first degree in the arts in my early twenties, I began my psychotherapy training. I got to meet the intellectually diverse at Regent's College and the intellectually intense at the Tavistock clinic; to me the training, although brilliant, seemed insular. The teaching did not really see the children in the context of socially depleted structures. It seemed as if the therapist once trained would require a client who ascribed to the theoretical ideal of the clinical boundary. To me the world described was a virtual world subject to fantasy controls.

I continued my personal analysis, completed the two-year Infant and Child Observation, my art psychotherapy foundation and my four-year psychotherapy M.A., and then I began my journey to work in the inner cities. My personal analysis continued five days a week for sixteen years; it acted as a sounding board at the most difficult times when I was creating the two charities. I also set up the counselling service for a university, and taught and worked there while training.

My first training placement was with the NSPCC Oxford Gardens, where assessments were carried out to ascertain if a parental abuser could be returned to the family home. Here I saw and learnt that the majority of abusers have been abused as children; here I learnt not to judge.

My first job was with a women's refuge. What devastation violence can cause, but it isn't as simple as "men hurt women". Whatever the theoretical explanation, the children in the playground at the refuge wept in their play. The poverty and the lack of resources was shocking. The women were cramped in tiny rooms, disturbed, their children stacked like goods on bunk bed shelves. The refuge workers were poorly paid, poorly trained and not therapeutically supervised. They tried hard, but the outcome was a neglectful service.

By my mid-twenties I was at Family Service Units. Full of aspirations, I decorated the dingy playroom space in the hope of helping children through therapeutic play. It was here that I understood the fundamental flaw in the provision of services to vulnerable children. The assumption is that behind every child is a responsible adult, who will navigate the path to services. The truth is that many of the children we were seeing didn't have an adult who could bring them to sessions. Many were being abused by their own carers and simultaneously silenced by them.

One December, an educational psychologist made a referral of a seven-year-old girl, who was trying to kill herself. She was wrapping a towel around her neck and covering her head with her plastic reading folder, hoping the lack of oxygen would lead to her death. She was jumping in front of cars and on a number of occasions had been seen on rooftops.

Just before Christmas, I visited the family home, a bleak space. The little seven-year-old was silent: tiny, blonde, frozen, with watchful eyes. But her mother could not bring her to therapy sessions. She had another child with special needs, who took up all her time. Using the suitcase of toys and art materials I had used with the children of the rich when I visited their homes, I decided to see this child in the school library. Our sessions had a peculiar silence about them. She used to draw unusual pictures: children's heads, and gorilla bodies; a distorted bird with a child's head. I remember feeling that something terrible was going to be disclosed, and the day came when she shared her secret.

Since the age of five she had been sexually abused by three men who lived in the tower block opposite. Every day this five-year-old had gone from her house to their house, and they had given her toys, but they were sexual ones. I remember feeling desperate as I realized that this child had had no one in her life to be able to share these events with. There was no one to speak to her, no one to listen to her story, and the horrors had been allowed to continue, to continue to the point of her wanting to kill herself.

As a result of child protection requirements I disclosed the contents of her conversations to social services and the police, and then I stood back and watched as she was re-traumatized through the process of disclosure. Medical examinations for which she was not prepared, and then a five-hour police disclosure interview during which words were used that she did not understand. The professionals decided eventually that she would not make a suitable witness. The seven-year-old would not be able to come up with a sequence of events, or attach dates and times to them. They wanted to spare her the humiliation of the court room, but they also devastated her by never honouring their promise to protect her or bring her abusers to justice.

One of the men was a postman. He delivered daily the post to her door. With every delivery, he was reminding her of how powerful he was. Eventually the men re-offended, this time with a twelve-year-old. But for the little seven-year-old girl who had placed her trust in all the grown-ups, the disappointment was too unbearable. She continued to self harm, to want to kill herself. In the end, for her own protection, the family moved to the country. I never saw her again but her experience fuelled me to set up The Place2Be, my first charity.

The school, realizing that they had let down their pupil, and wanting to achieve the best by its pupils, gave me a discarded broom cupboard to work in, which happened to have a window. As I was cleaning the room, I thought to myself, what shall I call it? And then I thought – "the place 2 be", somewhere where children can be safe to be children. At the time I was teaching at Regent's College, on the counselling and psychotherapy courses. I encouraged the students there to come down to South London and do their clinical work experience. With these first students came many others including those from different training schools. It turned out that this one therapy room led in time to many more in different schools.

I received a grant from several small foundations initially, and I re-mortgaged my flat, in order to ensure the survival of The Place2Be. One day I came out of my house to find the bailiffs standing outside. Abbey National had decided to take me to court, and I had not received a letter letting me know that this was the case. The bailiffs grinned!

I dashed to the court. The judge, a kindly gentleman, realized that I had used my money to set up a children's charity, and was both shocked and surprised. He told Abbey National he would not take my flat away, and eventually I paid them back.

In the same way Kids Company was created – using my mortgage and re-mortgaging. As The Place2Be took off, the government visited, suggesting that I turn it into a charity so that they could give me Department of Health and Education funding.

It was politically a tough time. The Child Psychotherapy Association didn't want me to set up in the inner cities in this way. They had a meeting to decide what to do, and after some deliberation they agreed to offer me support. But sometimes their support was toxic, their envy out of control. Some of the most senior people in the Association were extremely helpful because their career experiences had demonstrated to them that therapeutic support was sparse, and not accessible enough to poor inner-city children. At the time there were three-year waiting lists in child guidance in the inner cities, and children who desperately needed therapeutic intervention could not receive it.

After five years of setting up The Place2Be, when I was in my early thirties, I made the most painful decision of my life. I knew I had to leave in order to ensure the survival of The Place2Be.

Since then, its founding history has from time to time been airbrushed. It saddens me how my personal history is being rewritten, but an admirable job has been made of ensuring its continued survival and success.

In December 1996, when I left The Place2Be, I immediately founded Kids Company, using £20,000 donated to me by a local authority. I wanted to reach the most marginalized and the most disadvantaged. I was curious about the children who were not going to school.

My original intention was to take over some railway arches and renovate them, so that we could bring the children we were seeing for therapeutic support in the schools there during the holidays and look after them, then return them to school.

The railway arches in Camberwell were the birthplace of Kids Company. We took two arches at first. They were due to be opened from three to seven o'clock. We decorated them, anticipating that we would receive children from the schools, but the word spread on the streets, and in our early days, we ended up with about a hundred adolescent boys.

I remember those early days, I remember being so profoundly out of my depth. So terrified. I have the memory of the blood draining out of my cheeks, as I didn't know how to deal with this group. They in turn would arrive every day, sarcastic and curious. They would pull out little knives and rip the furniture and the fabrics. They would roll up their joints and burn their cigarettes into the chairs. I don't know what held me there, despite my terror. The only thing I remember is my Persian hospitality. At three o'clock, I would open the gate, welcome them, and ask them not to spit! They now tell me they found me fascinating, as I never retaliated, never shouted, and no matter what they did I kept opening the doors. Throughout this initial year I was greatly helped by Sue Reuben, who supported us financially and practically.

As time went on, approximately another hundred children, predominantly the children of drug addicts, arrived. Whereas the adolescent boys had been able to feed themselves through committing crimes, these younger ones were failing to thrive. We were seeing children gaunt with malnutrition, children who were losing their hair, children who were scavenging in bins. Nothing could have prepared me for the shock.

At first, I desperately tried to get social services involved, but I was hitting their thresholds all the time, and they were not taking the cases. At the time I could not understand why. But a number of years later someone explained to me that the children I was referring, who were suffering from neglect and being left without food, were not eligible for support, because social services were so under-resourced and snowed under with cases of sexual and physical abuse. I suddenly understood why the eleven-year-old who called social services desperate about the fact that there was no food in the cupboard was not getting the help. As I visited social services and read these children's files I realized the neglect and abuse they were experiencing was chronic.

I cried. Sometimes I felt so exhausted, and at night, I felt overwhelmed by the burden of what I had started. But at no time did I ever contemplate giving up, because in front of me, every day, were examples of tremendous courage. These children who struggled to survive. And as I got to know them, they began telling me their life stories, and I began writing them down. They were horrific stories of young children battered, shot at, beaten, hurled to the wall as parents struggled with drug withdrawal. These were children who, in order to survive, had become drug couriers or drug-dealers. Some were doing bank robberies, some were making £4000 a week and sharing it among the whole group. And these were children who could not be returned to school, who'd been out of education for a number of years. Seventeen-year-olds who were capable of killing but could not write their names or addresses.

I struggled against the local authority as the local authority became aware of my witnessing the real statistics. Sixty per cent of the first hundred who had arrived had not been in education, and no one had gone looking for them. No one wanted them back. Their behaviour and emotional difficulties put pressure on the school classroom, and teachers were only too glad to lose them.

Those early days, I didn't even understand a word the children said. I didn't understand their street language, their criminal network, and very early on I realized that I had to employ some males from the community who could interpret the children's world and who could support us. They were exceptional people who joined the company, but they were people who had had no education, no training, no history of employment. They had tremendous natural capacities to deal with the children who had arrived, but they also had difficulties in being honest, in turning up on time, and in understanding therapeutic thinking.

I had ended up with a workforce made up of qualified therapists, trained in the schools of Hampstead, and unqualified workers who were brilliant with the children. In the beginning the only thing these two workforces had in common was their combined hatred of the children. The children made them angry and rageful. The children trod on their dignity as their own dignity had been trodden on. The children terrorized them as they had been terrorized, and we struggled every day for some safe control.

There were several key transition points in the provision of the service. The first of these was when we offered an evening meal, which we did not charge the children for. This felt as if it was a significant milestone in the development of the organization. The children thought us different from other provisions, because we were engaging in an act of care without asking for something back for it. Then we began providing bus passes and living allowances to the most disadvantaged. In this way, we were addressing the core problems of poverty which were driving the children into criminal activity.

An environment of trust developed at the Arches. Young people now knew that they could turn to us and we were prepared to stand by them. In the meantime I struggled to develop therapeutic thinking and practices and to develop services which would meet the needs of these youngsters in appropriate ways. The biggest hurdle that I encountered was lack of funding. Because the children and young people were self-referring, they were not arriving at our door with pots of money attached to them. When we went back to social services, to try to see that their basic needs were met, we were told often it would be best if we didn't find these children in the first place as the local authority's budget could not cope. We faced the same challenges as the children – adult drug addicts and dealers who attempted to shoot us and drove a car onto our premises to run over the children or who arrived with knives to stab us.

We struggled against other people's prejudices. We were at one point removed from our premises due to corruptions and injustices. Very very few of the parents of the 125 children who were reliant on our evening meals and came to us from the immediate streets, dared to stand up and say their children needed this service. The most shocking part of our eviction from our premises was the fact that not a single politician and just one council official stood by these children (the Director of Children's Social Services in Southwark submitted a letter of support). No one seemed keen to see what would happen to the children if the lifeline of Kids Company was severed. I had to go as far as the Court of Appeal trying to represent the approximately 500 children using the service at the time.

History will set the record straight. It will all come out in the wash. The children were evicted on the grounds of loss of amenities to the residents. Someone forgot that the children were residents too. That injustice compounded my resolve to stand by the children.

Eventually we were given other premises thanks to Lambeth Council and Granada TV, who generously renovated a once derelict warehouse for us. A firm of builders, Interior and Exterior, carried out and paid for all the refurbishment and they continued to support us with other projects.

Kids Company nearly closed on several occasions. The staff here were so dedicated, they refused to leave. Eventually, after the politicking, the raising awareness, and the appearing in the media, we were offered a £3.4 million grant (over three years and only if we matched it with our own fundraising from businesses and individuals) from the Treasury in April 2005, to enable us to replicate our model of practice.

This is the stage at which I'm writing this book, and I'm writing it because there are fundamental flaws in the way we treat children and the way our services are structured. The services unwittingly discriminate against the disadvantaged, and especially against children who do not have a competent carer in their lives.

We currently have a culture in which threat delivers the best resources. If someone threatens the local authority with solicitors, then they are likely to get a statement of special educational needs for their child. We knew the threat of legal action worked. In one year we had to take local authorities to the doors of courts thirty-three times, because they would not house children for whom they were responsible. We won on every single occasion, or they settled before we got to the courtroom. But if you're a child on your own in the inner cities or in an isolated farmhouse, if you are being abused behind closed doors, no one will notice you, no one will know until you're old enough to protest – to make your rage visible. And then the injustice is that they do not admit to the damage that has been caused. Instead they want to punish the child for what in effect is the adults' failure to care.

As I write this book, Kids Company continues its services in twenty-five schools across London, reaching some 4500 children through therapeutic and social work services. At its children's centre it offers a comprehensive and holistic service to some 600 children a year who turn to it from the street.

Often people ask what are our successes? What are our outcomes? I want to tell them the truth, because the lies that keep being told distort the service provision and harm children further. The truth is that very disturbed children take a very long time to provide visible outcomes. Their outcomes are personal, and their successes are often individual and emotional first, before they become visible in the world of academia and work.

The child who has been sexually abused, who originally used to freeze rigid when you sat next to him, may embrace you or put his arm next to you, allowing his skin your touch. That is a successful outcome. The child who was frenzied, could not sit still, who initiated action in order to avoid feeling, that child being able to sit for ten minutes quietly, that's a successful outcome.

We have many, many successful outcomes which stem from vulnerable children's valiant struggle to survive abuse. They may not be visible in the league tables, and people may not value them, but the truth is that before an educational outcome there needs to be an emotional one. Many of our children go on to succeed educationally. This year, many acquired qualifications. Some got three A-levels. Some received distinctions from their colleges. But it took five, maybe six years, to get children who had been emotionally damaged to the point where they could succeed academically.

The problem with presenting outcomes in the way that they are being demanded is that clinicians try and exclude children from their services who are likely not to provide positive outcomes. This is not because the clinician is cruel, it's because the clinician will be deprived of money if he doesn't give the government the outcomes the government is expecting.

What kind of a service have we ended up developing? Why are we driven by economic and perverse ideals, which in effect don't reflect the kind of provision that is needed for the most damaged and fragile? Children who have experienced extreme neglect and damage do not produce outcomes the way we expect them. Nevertheless, their success is palpable. They are dignified individuals who are making their way back from emotionally dark places.

The youngsters may not be Olympic heroes or business leaders, because their starting point was so much more horrific. Their medals should be given to them because they're surviving their experience of childhood. Because they battle every day against the will to commit suicide. Every day they balance the struggle between wanting to die and struggling to live.

These are amazing children and we owe it to them to honour them, to recognize what's happening to them, and to take responsibility for the fact that once damage has been caused within their family home, we are not advanced enough, developed enough, or honourable enough as a society to protect them through corporate parenting. Our social care structures are doing a bad job. Staff within them are demoralized, and they suffer from a poverty of vision. They are being forced to mimic business values, when they went into the profession with an emotional vocation. We owe it to these teams to give them back their will to carry out their care with a restored sense of vocation and positive aspirations.

I hope that in reading these letters you will see the struggles the children embrace. You will see how the myth of an intervention leading to a positive outcome is misleading, and that the truth is there are many beginnings, many failures, and some small successes.

I hope that we will have the wisdom not to undermine these achievements of our children, and to respect them for the strength and determination they have shown. We shouldn't punish, humiliate, and hide children who have already had their childhood diminished.

Many of the young people who listened to these letters cried, quietly, their tears honourable, gently dripping off their cheeks. For once their experience was reflected back as they saw it and they received an apology long due to them.

Someone should have cherished their childhood. The least they deserve is the truth.

CHAPTER 2

Introduction
to Therapeutic Thinking

PSYCHOTHERAPISTS, COUNSELLORS, PSYCHOANALYSTS and psychologists train to acquire a better understanding of human interaction. For the purpose of clarity, I have defined their training parameters in this chapter and their favoured methods of working, so that readers unfamiliar with therapy can acquire a basic understanding of this field. I will refer to the group collectively as therapeutic thinkers and outline how they share the same ideology.

Therapeutic thinkers and their shared philosophy

All therapeutic thinkers believe experiences in childhood to be fundamental in creating emotional and behavioural repertoires in adulthood. Central to the formation of character is the intense relationship with the caregiver/mother. It is universally accepted in the childcare professions that infants, in order to thrive emotionally and physically, require a well-attuned maternal experience. "Attunement" is achieved when the significant caregiver (the person who acts in a maternal capacity) is sensitive to the child's needs, responds empathically, warmly, and mirrors the infant appropriately. The milestone needing to be achieved is one of attachment between carer and child. If the attachment relationship is robust and sensitive, the child develops a sense of security. If the attachment is inconsistent and unpredictable and is not in tune with the infant's needs, the child develops an ambivalent or insecure attachment. Some children, like Romanian orphans who were brought up in institutions and received minimal mothering, are left with an incapacity or poor capacity to form attachments. Major areas of their brain development are thought to be affected as a result of the unavailability of a significant carer in their lives, who could mirror them and be attuned with them. Some go on as a result of this deprivation to develop aggressive and violent behaviours.

Initially, infants are reliant on the carer for survival, but as time goes on and the child becomes more independent of the mother physically, there is greater presence of the mother figure mentally. The child "internalizes" (incorporates into their thinking and feeling) the mother figure and calls upon the memory of care she had given in order to self-soothe or self-motivate. The capacity to internalize care-giving and to begin thinking psychologically about care and relationships is often referred to as the ability to "mentalize" or "mentalization". Fathers also play an important role in looking after the mother and facilitating the child's link to the external world.

A child's identity and self-esteem are fundamentally dependent on parental perception and the way the child perceives the parent's responses as he grows up. Not all care situations are ideal or satisfactory all the time. Sometimes, carers fail to be empathic to their children's needs. At the mild end, parents may act out onto the child their own fears, anxieties and sometimes they fail in being appropriate in their responses. No therapeutic thinker expects parental carers to be perfect. However, if they are "good enough" and on the whole nurturing to their children, the overall outcome is likely to be positive. The fact that parents sometimes are good in their care and sometimes they fall short may actually facilitate resilience in the child, enabling the child to tolerate frustration without falling apart. However, the shortcoming in the care must not be overwhelming or catastrophic, or the infant will be left in a state of feeling they might not survive the experience as chronic lack of care is tremendously destructive and does not lead to resilience.

To protect themselves against emotional pain, children develop strategies in order to avoid painful feelings generated by failure to care. In therapeutic thinking, these are referred to as "defence mechanisms". All human beings have defences which are intended as protective of their emotional lives. Some children may choose to forget bad experiences, others may deny they ever took place. Some children rush around in a frenzied way in order to avoid having time to think, in case a bad feeling emerges. Some children distract themselves by focusing their attention on something else, for example, eating or not eating, so that the feeling that is really bothering them is not allowed attention. Sometimes defences and anxieties are hidden in other activities. They are "symbolized". Defence mechanisms are considered a useful tool for emotional survival. They allow a human being to maintain a sense of dignity and only to face what they can cope with. However, sometimes an old defence is no longer useful, because life has, in reality, moved on. A child who was being abused by an uncle may have needed to avoid him, in order not to be subjected to violence, and may have hated the relative. If this child goes on to hate all adult men and avoid relating to them, then the defence mechanism becomes provocative and self-destructive. A therapeutic thinker would spend time talking and exploring the original trauma, which resulted in the defence being needed and then help the child to consider new ways of behaving in relation to contact with non-abusing males.

Exploring of events and their emotional impact is often referred to as "working through". There is a suggestion that experiences that have not been processed or worked through accumulate energy around them, which then preoccupies the child and does not allow him to use the psychological energy constructively elsewhere.

Talking through a problem is like releasing steam from a kettle that has been boiling. It is a relief, although the process of doing it may be challenging, often reminding the individual of what the original pain felt like. Children who have a fairly solid sense of themselves and good internal emotional resources can benefit from talking and working through their problems. Often such children make good use of group therapy or counselling and they are able to work on specific issues, leading to a resolution and a restoration of balance. The assumption with this type of child is that their personality is relatively stable and intact, because they have been, on the whole, parented appropriately. There has been sufficient attunement and sufficient understanding of their needs. The process of infant–carer attachment has been allowing the child to develop a healthy attachment relationship to their carer.

A healthy attachment is now understood to be the foundation of mental health. Therapeutic thinkers believe that whatever soothing, calming, interested and loving behaviour the maternal carer demonstrates towards the child, the child internalizes these and makes use of them later. The attachment also allows recovery from any potential emotional pain. It is as if the brain has become resilient as a result of the loving relationship and any subsequent traumatic events are likely to be overcome. The internalization of the care-relationship is often referred to as "object relation" (also known as internal maps or Personal Constructs). It means that your understandings of mother, father and other significant relationships become part of your psychological thinking. Your mind acquires an inner mother and father, which helps you to "self-parent" just as you were externally parented by your carers.

Object relation and internalization are essential prerequisites for maturity. Infants learn to tolerate gaps between the time they have contact with their parents and their parents' absence. If the attachment is good and the child has internalized the good care construct, then his tolerance of parental absence is higher and less persecutory. The child has some good inner resources enabling him to remember that the parent is kind and loving, to believe she will return, and, above all, to understand that in the meantime he himself has inner resources and memories of the care given which he can use to soothe himself. The inner parental figures establish ways of relating to others, hence object relations. A boy treated badly by his mother may have internalized a negative image of females, which may impact on how he relates to his female boss. These object relations are generated in infancy and childhood, and they have an impact on how you relate as an adult to others and how you deal with your problems.

The importance of attachment was first identified by John Bowlby in the 1960s, who also identified different styles of attachment. Sometimes attachment relationships can go wrong. A child may have had carers whose care giving is inconsistent. Consequently "ambivalent attachment" behaviour is created in the child. The child can see himself as not worthy of help or love. The carer who constantly avoids care responsibility and rejects the child may force the infant into an "avoidant attachment" model, whereby the child avoids connection to people and is excessively self-reliant. The disorganized caregiver ("disorganized attachment") may frighten the child, resulting in reactions of anger which is poorly controlled.

Some children may also experience the loss of a parent through separation or death. This can have a catastrophic impact on their subsequent development, depending at what age the loss happened. It is thought that if they occur during infancy and adolescence these losses lead to significant disturbances.

Therapeutic thinkers also agree that human beings have different developmental needs at different stages, both as children growing up, and in terms of life stages. Abraham Maslow, also a psychologist, produced a very simple analysis of needs hierarchies, which therapeutic thinkers accept as appropriate. Maslow believed that unless some basic needs were met, the more spiritual and intellectual needs could not be appropriately addressed. So, if you are desperately hungry you are more likely to be preoccupied with finding food to eat than with writing poetry. Maslow divided his needs into a triangle of needs, as in the figure below, with the physiological being given basic priority and self-actualization being the ultimate goal.

For therapy to be effective, the meeting of basic needs must, on the whole, be facilitated first. It is worth noticing that Maslow's triangle organizes needs-satisfaction in a way that is not too dissimilar to the way in which the brain is organized, with physiological needs being genetically programmed and controlled by the more primitive structures of the brain; affiliative (social) needs being facilitated through nurture, family and attachment, while self-actualization allows for greater independence and capacity for compassion, which are located within the less primitive structures and functions of the brain, primarily around the frontal lobe.

Most people face challenges in life and overcome them. Some grapple with these difficulties with greater anxiety. They are often referred to as experiencing neurosis (I can't stand the word!). Neurosis is anxiety, which is relevant but exaggerated, and not delusional.

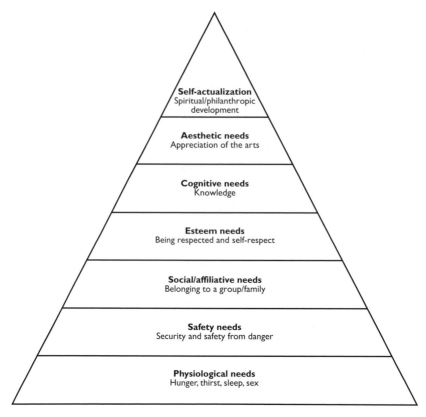

Maslow's hierarchy of needs

Others face greater challenges which stem from mental health difficulties. Some mental health difficulties are entrenched, not as a result of biochemical disturbances, but as the products of disturbed upbringings. It is thought that they are created as a result of poor interactions between carers and their children. Therapeutic thinkers refer to these difficulties as "personality disorders". Personality disorders are not deemed to be treatable, but can be managed to cause least problems for clients and those who come into contact with them. The most severe personality disorder is thought to be sociopathology, which is socially expressed without the individual having genuine access to regret, remorse or compassion. Sometimes sociopaths are violent or engage in fraudulent activities. In children, the most common type of personality disorders are deemed to be disorders of conduct, in which behaviours are aggressive and poorly managed.

"Conduct disorders" seems to be an umbrella diagnosis for a lot of childhood behaviour difficulties. Some would argue that this is lazy diagnosis on the part of psychiatrists who do not enquire more deeply.

Some mental illnesses are chemically provoked. These include severe anxiety, depression or other mood disorders. Usually these conditions respond well to medication and some individuals can recover from them after a period of time.

Other mental illnesses, however, are more chronic, for example, schizophrenia, which is classed as a "psychosis", whereby the individual has a weak grip on reality. Currently, a large number of hospitals are filled with individuals who suffer from psychosis (a loss of touch with reality) as a result of significant substance misuse. Psychosis requires medical intervention for equilibrium to be maintained. Some recover from it. Others have to manage it with medication and if they cease using their medication, they are returned to a state of psychosis from a state of equilibrium.

Therapeutic and medical practitioners diagnose mental illness using a universal dictionary of diagnosis called *Diagnostic and Statistical Manual of Mental Disorders*, produced by the American Psychiatric Association. In this way, there is a common understanding and vocabulary of conditions shared amongst therapeutic and medical professionals.

Children can have special challenges, which are developmentally identified. These could include communication disorders, such as childhood autism or language and speech processing disorders, as well as disorders of attention and activity, where there is hyperactivity or an inability to manage energy levels.

To modify object relations, or ways of perceiving and acting on the world, therapeutic thinkers adopt two strategies. Those schools of thought believing "rational thought" to be the seed of change adopt cognitive strategies to modify object relations. The cognitive practitioner believes "faulty thinking" can be modified if it is explored and the client can understand how the behaviour is redundant and inappropriate under current circumstances. The cognitive therapist would explore the feelings and thoughts which lead to the origins of the behaviour, for example, what was it that your mother did that made you dislike her? They will then point out how "irrational" it is to believe all women are like the client's mother in their behaviour. This understanding is thought to facilitate change according to cognitive strategies of therapeutic intervention. Sometimes cognitive therapists may engage in helping the client change their behaviour through the process of "behaviour therapy" whereby good and life enhancing actions are given positive feedback and the redundant ones are given negative feedback in the hope that lack of reward will lead to the behaviour stopping. In getting the client to do things differently they may facilitate learning through practice.

Other therapeutic thinkers believe simply pointing out the "faulty thinking" does not bring about change in the client's perception. They believe object relations are emotionally constructed and can only be modified through the provision of an alternative emotional experience. The therapeutic thinker then provides an alternative relationship for the client. At first, the client transfers to the therapist their feelings about their "original mother". In the transference the therapist sees and understands the client's relationship to their mother, and through the process of counter-transference (the therapist's own feelings), the therapist acquires an understanding of how the client's mother may have felt towards him and how the client perceived the impact. Using the relationship between client and therapeutic worker, the practitioner uses the feeling displayed by the child and her own self-awareness in order to acquire an understanding of the concerns experienced by the client. Some aspects of this care-relationship also serve to bring about modifications or change in the client's ways of relating (their object relation). As time goes on, the client may intraject (take in) the care given by the therapeutic worker and use this to enhance and strengthen their positive object relations or to change negative constructs. Whether approaching the therapeutic encounter from a cognitive or object relation perspective, ultimately the outcome is affording the child a greater ability to relate to others more constructively and approach life with less need to defend against it.

There are numerous philosophies of therapy, each with a different construct on how emotions work, but there are more similarities than differences between the approaches. Many share a fundamental set of beliefs in common. These include the importance of dreams in revealing what the subconscious is preoccupied with, as well as the central role played by defence mechanisms. The personality is thought to operate through two levels of consciousness. One is more evident to the individual, therefore referred to as conscious, i.e. the person knows what they feel and why. The other is thought to be unconscious, which means that the awareness is more disguised from the individual's consciousness.

Often therapeutic workers believe that unconscious material may use up psychological energy in being kept hidden from consciousness, but also it may influence behaviour leaving the client unaware of why she acted or reacted in a certain way. Some thinkers believe that material from the unconscious initially becomes available in pre-consciousness and then becomes conscious. This basically means that gently the client becomes aware of material existing that was previously completely hidden to her, that she may not have fully become aware of its content until she becomes completely conscious of it. It is as if there is a ball of wool that is completely hidden in the cupboard and no one knows where it is, hence "unconscious". Then the ball of wool is discovered and you can see strands coming from it, hence pre-conscious. And then finally, someone pulls the ball of wool apart, making the various strands visible, and that is consciousness. Therapeutic thinkers believe that making the client aware of unconscious content is helpful in enhancing self-awareness and contributes to clients taking more responsibility for their behaviour. The unconscious is often revealed in dreams or mistakes, referred to as "Freudian slips" or even jokes, as well as behaviour, play and sometimes artistic expression.

The arts are a useful tool in therapy. Some practitioners train specifically to use the arts as a form of psychotherapy. The advantage of the arts is that the client and therapist can explore emotional issues through symbolic expressions.

Symbolic expression is when an image or a piece of action expresses some feeling or thought, without directly being involved in the thoughts or feelings. The original thought is represented by an alternative expression, almost disguised.

Sometimes this can feel less persecutory for the client, as the image both objectifies and helps disguise feelings or thought, affording the client sufficient distance to feel safe in exploring the concern. The arts are also very releasing of emotional energy, enabling access to physiological pathways which may not be so easily accessed through words.

Current fields of therapeutic use of the arts include art psychotherapy, dance movement therapy, music therapy, psychodrama, drama therapy.

Drama and play therapy are especially effective with children because they enable them to disguise concerns through symbolization or role play, and they also enable the practice of new strategies or ways of behaving. So drama and play therapy are both expressive and an opportunity to rehearse new ways of being.

There are also schools of therapy which specifically focus on "body work". Their understanding of working through problems stems from the belief that emotions and memories are physically stored. When they are allowed a release at a physiological level, the necessary mental changes are mobilized. This process is in reverse, based on the idea that the body has the capacity to bring about changes in thinking, whereas most therapeutic interventions are based on the idea that thinking has the capacity to bring about changes in physical action.

Conclusion

Therapeutic thinkers aim to restore to the client the ability to function in a pro-social and personally fulfilling way. To achieve this, both client and therapist work through inappropriate defences, modify object relations and generate conditions in which satisfactory attachments are facilitated. Their ultimate task is to help the client to access love and meaning in their lives.

CHAPTER 3

Exploring the Impact of Sexual Abuse

Letter to Chardonnay

THIS LETTER IS to a young girl who was horrifically sexually abused by her father and other men, and subsequently raped by drug dealers. Often children who have been abused seek to abuse themselves and others in a form of self-hatred and revenge. Overwhelming feelings often seek suppression through the use of mind-altering substances and children may use drugs or drink, or both, to reduce flashbacks of abuse, and diminish feelings of emotional pain. Medical and psychiatric interventions can be experienced as repeating the abuse. At times, the victim seeks to regain mastery over previously overwhelming feelings by behaving like an abuser, either towards themselves or others.

Children who have been violently abused can present with murderous feelings. If controls are poor the client could cause harm to others. They may also turn the murderous feelings onto themselves in attempted suicides and significant self-harm. Children who have been sexually abused may present with complex attitudes to sexuality. They may behave in a promiscuous way, but disassociate themselves from the behaviour. They may be terrified of sexual contact and not be able to integrate loving feelings into sexual encounters. They may be phobic of sexuality, while simultaneously promiscuous.

The sexual abuse of this young girl began when she was ten years old. Her father betrayed her by facilitating it, and her mother compounded the hurt by not protecting her. Her mother continued to cruelly reject her. The ambivalent and destructive mother–child relationship has made recovery for this young girl an even greater challenge. Often professionals, sensing the desperation of circumstances, would act inappropriately on a counter-transference experience. Because they were professionally and institutionally paralyzed, the psychiatric and social services at times behaved, unwittingly, as abusers and victims, creating greater desolation in the young girl.

Violent sexual abuse in childhood continues to have ramifications in adult life, the power of the conscious memory of the assault may diminish but this memory can still permeate all other experiences. Clients may need extensive therapeutic help to differentiate between the abuse and current encounters and relationships.

The greatest damage is to the capacity for trust and authenticity. The self begins to hide in order not to suffer further assault on its integrity. Yet the price is the loss of emotional truth. Somewhere behind the intellectual discourses and explanations of violence, exaggerated power and denial, is the littleness that once risked trusting, and yearns to do it again. The child seeks reunion with the safe maternal experience as part of the healing process. Yet excessive defences make it difficult for therapeutic workers to help the violently abused child.

As clinicians you must not give up. Every step gained creates hope against suicidal self-destruction. Your care is resilience building, even if it can't take the pain away.

I asked her what she wanted to be called in this letter. She replied Chardonnay. Her dignity was preserved in choosing to be a wine rather than a girl. The drink symbolized her defiance.

DEAR CHARDONNAY,

I first came across you when you lay flat on your belly, relentlessly slamming your face onto the pavement. I sat beside you putting my hands between your forehead and the concrete, cushioning you against the blows. You could not feel the physical pain, because your emotional hurt had reached inexplicable despair. Your cry was desperate, devastated, and I was left silent, wondering what horrors had reduced you to such levels of self-destruction. Your little arms had lines of terror torn into them. Every inch of their skin scarred by your self-hatred.

You never spoke, only terrorized. You seemed only to torment others. I had heard of your rage, your cruelty, your ability to seek a victim and then humiliate them. The staff were terrified and tired as, every day, they negotiated the storm of your spirit.

I sat there next to you on that pavement, deeply aware of the magnitude of your pain. I knew unspeakable horrors lurked beneath, and yet I knew nothing. People walked by, some perplexed, others knowingly sympathetic. Night spread its blanket, and yet I had nothing which could comfort you. This deep and devastated cry of yours, I would hear many more times. Each time I questioned if the pain would ever go away.

The following day, you seemed withdrawn and exhausted. You sat opposite me rigid. The space between us was like a magnet. You wanted proximity, and yet you resisted as a wall of mistrust kept you frozen in your chair. I came closer, afraid of the risk I was about to take. Could I really enter your devastated space bearing promises of gentleness? Or would you experience me as a persecutor and expel me with your deadly fury.

Your little face was so deeply yearning, childlike and vigilant. I sat next to you, relieved that you did not escape the closeness. "Only children who have had something terrible happen to them cry like you did last night." You looked right through me and I felt like weeping as your glance penetrated my being with pain too unbearable to describe. I could feel no words could explain what you needed to tell. It was too deeply embedded. The uttering of it felt like it would murder you. "If you can't tell me in words, try drawing it for me. I will do my best to understand." Your breathing generated panic, and yet despite the visible terror, you picked up the paper and drew. Men with guns, with chains, beds, a little girl, and then you stopped. You had gone too far, revealed too much. The risk felt unbearable. I had to guess the rest, but I knew I could not tell it before you had.

The next time you completed your horrific history was a Sunday afternoon. I received a desperate call from you, asking for a meeting. As I was in the West End of London, we agreed to meet at a nearby hotel, in posh Park Lane! When I arrived, you were standing trance-like in the middle of the busy road, waiting to be run over. You seemed so still. So oblivious to the danger. So mindless and serene. I shouted to get your attention. Humour seemed to be the only weapon against your deadliness: "Can you leave the suicide for after tea?" You grinned. The surreal always surpassed the real in an inexplicable way. Many a time, this humorous exchange returned both of us to your living from the edge of your wish for death.

You sat as they brought the pristine white china, with your street-wear and glowing skin, a stranger to the space. You were too full, too desperate to talk, and then you began dragging the unbearable words out of your mouth. With each word, your legs shook. You dragged your fingers through your cheeks, as if to peel the hatred off your face. With each word revealing your pain, you sought to inflict damage to yourself. I was terrified about being able to contain the situation. The waiting staff and other guests could feel the oppressive state you had reached. You were holding back fierce tears as if crying would be defeat. Your perfect white teeth ripped your lips, biting back the emotions. The tension felt too dangerous. I signaled the staff to find me a more private space away from the gaze of the other guests.

We ended up in the hallway of a ballroom, and you began again slamming your little head against the wall with a force too foul to describe. It was relentless, your muscles became too powerful with hatred, and I could sense the power of your self-harm, unleashing devastating destruction. I had to wrestle you to the ground and hold you in my arms on the floor. I was scared of the abyss we had both entered.

The abuse you experienced is horrific – they invaded every space possible with violation too obscene to describe in this letter.

For days after the disclosure, all you wanted to do was tear open your skin. Blood seemed to be better at weeping than tears. You couldn't cry for you didn't value yourself enough to feel compassion for yourself. The abuse felt like a well-deserved trophy for the disgust you felt you embodied. I was exhausted as I watched your every move. Sharp objects had acquired a murderous attraction. You hit broken glass, sharp discarded objects, and triumphantly dragged them into your arms and belly. The cutting delivered momentary relief as you followed the blood weaving a red thread of release out of your flesh. I could only beg you to help me keep it safe. It was as though you wanted me to know how powerless you felt, as I watched like an incompetent bystander while you assumed the role of abuser in relation to yourself.

The information you had given me felt too devastating to hold on to on my own. The men were still around. I wondered if they had access to other children. Your mother knew nothing, and yet through-out these years you had both been attending clinics for your challeng-ing behaviour and the fractious relationship between the two of you.

I asked your permission to share your disclosure with social services, and your psychiatrist. You courageously allowed me, despite the tremendous humiliation. You had spent years terrorizing the clinic workers and they lived believing your bad behaviour to be symptom-atic of a label, "conduct disorder". I felt sad that so much expertise and education had not afforded them enough curiosity to seek meaning in your maddening behaviour.

When I went to share the disclosure, they refused to allow me to speak. They wanted you to tell them in your own words for child pro-tection purposes, and yet they were terrified of how dangerously you might behave in the process. They could not guarantee your safety, the safety of the workers, or the safety of the perpetrators. The terror acted upon you was now spreading like a virus through all those profession-als who needed to help.

To this day I carry the details of the secret with you. The self-destruction which had been a feature of your existence had now gained momentum. From the age of eleven you had been on the streets with other similarly violated children. Sometimes sleeping on the streets, sometimes on the beaches and other people's floors. Every sanctuary you sought delivered perverse opportunities for damage. You described with profound empathy and guilt how an eleven-year-old boy was taken for sweets by an older man in Brighton, and then returned to the group devastated after being raped in the grave-yard.

Aged twelve, after all the devastating trauma, you sought sanctuary in another child's home. Social services never checked them out, yet they were offered £50 a week to look after you. The money was spent on the parents' addictions, as you and the other children shared the floor with rats. Not a single chair, sheets that looked like they had not seen the wash for a decade. Images on the duvet on the bed intended to evoke a loved childhood were suffocated beneath the dirt. Each child had a half bin liner full of clothes on the floor – their entire worldly possessions. There were no cupboards where you could hang your clothes. Even the kitchen cupboard doors swung off their hinges in desperation. Windows were boarded up or broken. What responsible authority deems such a space worthy as a sanctuary for such vulnerable children?

You saw many horrors when you should have been offered safety. All of you children survived by doing robberies, stealing. In fact, this was the first time our staff came across you. Your need for help always communicated itself through your capacity for inflicting terror. You wanted to rob one of our teachers, but she didn't give in and then she recognized your vulnerability and suggested that you contact Kids Company. She explained where you could find us. Your response, "nobody can cope with me ". Such a sad and true statement. At times, I wondered if I could cope with you too.

Your rage seemed so random, so relentless and unforgiving. You broke things, hurled chairs, battered staff, bottled people, carried knives. Every benign object in the service of your terror acquired dangers we had never anticipated. After these bouts of inexplicable rage, where you inflicted the devastation within onto the canvas of our lives, exhausted, you would weep. That uncontrollable gut churning cry, which seemed never to find solace.

Your shame and regret were greater retributions than we could ever wish for you. So many times you attempted to take your own life – swallowing pills, digging death into your own arms, and even running in front of buses for the delivery of suicide. The local hospitals didn't even want you. Accident and emergency departments would declare alert when you arrived. The staff knew you, and were exhausted by your self-hate and hatred for others. When they rang around to find you beds on general or psychiatric wards, no one wanted you. You were aware of this rejection. You watched them as they tried to pass on the responsibility, plead with managers to accommodate you. For hours you would wait in emergency, hoping someone would offer you the sanctuary you needed.

I watched in despair and horror as they placed you in so-called "safe spaces", where beneath the professionalism lurked even more perverse dangers. The high security ward of a hospital where more crack cocaine and street drugs were available than you could ever find on the streets. Desolate patients gazed vacuously into the neutrality of the vanilla walls, blending into them. Sometimes the rage of a patient would punctuate the morbidity. The woman who pursued every patient with obscenities. The grown men who would behave in terrifying and sexualized ways, plunging you back into the realm of your childhood abuse with flashbacks which had no mercy.

Your little childlike face was vigilant with childish terror in this crazy and unforgiving space. The boredom had no alternatives. It dragged the minutes into a lingering spiritual death. What healing lay in this ward? Where was the peace, the containment? Even the tranquillizing drugs were injected unjustly into you, to silence your protest. Your childlike fantasy perceived the security men to be emerging from beneath the floor out of a secret hide-out. The alarm would ring and big men would wrestle you to the ground. Subject you to the indignity of a jab into your buttocks. How were you to see these men as your healers, and not representing the men who abused you and locked you up, as they rendered you powerless with their masculine supremacy? You were too small then to fight back, and too small now to resist. The hate internalized, sat in its trenches to be unleashed in some revenge further on in the day. You never forgot. Even if the drugs reduced your muscles to plasticity. Beneath the enforced calm, the paralysis of your spirit, lurked memory of this injustice. It waited for the next explosive opportunity to expel itself. And so your days passed, mindless, pointless, in this perverse place, masquerading as a mental health intervention.

They never really talked to you. They were so sure these experts that they had the answers. The combined intellect of men and women who had had the opportunity to be educated. The doctors who had credited themselves with psychiatric accolades. They were so careless. They did not care, and they cared even less to seek the truth. The diagnostic manual did the thinking for them. You could be found on its pages under "conduct disorder". It seemed enough this label. It allowed them not to face their own humanity or yours.

Somehow you were deemed to be different. They didn't have the humility to understand that they had just been lucky, that they didn't tear themselves and wound the walls in despair, like you did, because they had just been lucky. Lucky not to be abused as a little girl and overpowered. Their sense of potency was intact. They had not experienced the hideous devastation you had dragged yourself back from time and time again.

The ward was dirty. The room bare for safety. The mattress a piss-protected plastic. The windows had bars, and as the inmates could not escape, they peeled their dreams from off the walls. Behind the radiator, the dirt held every inmate's history. Years of it rested triumphantly undiscovered. Even the sun rejected the room, just a bleak yawn to burden the air. I cried for you but could not lift the Section, which made this your new home.

Your mother visited once and took off you the money I had left for the payphone. She brought no gift, and yet you gifted her. Your loyalty has always been awe-inspiring. You forgave her more than her bitterness would allow her to forgive. What damage had made her so cold and so cruel? Time and time again I was a witness to your phone calls to her, as you desperately sought to be her child again. You begged her. You, who would not beg even when a knife was at your throat. You pleaded with her, like a desperate child, to have you just on Christmas Day. For one night to sleep in her house. But she didn't want you at her house.

There could never be words to console. If only your mother knew how much you protected her. How you never told social services and health workers how she maltreated you. You spared her feelings of guilt and envy, by never telling her the extent to which we were helping you. You always wanted to feel that her position as your mother was sacred, protected and preserved for her return. Every little sign which could promise a reunion between the two of you would infuse you with hope, and then would come the realization of it being an illusion, trampling your happiness back into nothing.

Often you were torn between all the mothers you had mobilized to care for you. Yet you lived in the bosom of chaos. Piles of clothes merged with piles of desolate children scavenged for maternity. What was I in your life? A therapist with genuine love for you or a toxic abuser like all others? Did I really want the best for you? Or was I enslaving you in another form of self-satisfaction? Was my brand of healing a disguised abuse, like so many you had experienced before? How could you tell the difference? Against what sane barometer of normality could any of us be measured up for your judgment? Where was there some surviving good in you for you to be able to call upon? Sometimes it felt the good in you had been too devastated.

Sometimes I hated you, as I felt disbelief at the harm you had initiated upon another. Sometimes I felt bullied by you, trapped as your victim. You, like the abusers, had the upper hand. You could hit, spit, and destroy, when I could not resort to the same. You knew my control always made me weaker than you, but I had a greater weapon in our battles for sanity. I cared. And my caring was something you valued. The relationship between us felt sometimes like a tempestuous sea. Your storms could be too overpowering, and at times I felt exhaustion would drown us both. Sometimes I despaired, as I could not see the way ahead. You were lethal in your self-loathing and childlike in your logic. If you were unhappy then an innocent passer-by who had a smile had to "have it wiped off their face", so that you could grin in excitement as they took on your feelings of being victimized, and you'd triumphed in making a shift from victim to perpetrator. You were a smile thief as well as a robber of possessions.

I always needed to remind you of your goodness, of your compassion, so that you didn't deem yourself too unworthy to be protected against the harm you could cause. Sometimes in despair you wished yourself dead and believed prison was the only destination willing to offer you a legitimate resting place.

In your darkest moments another attempted suicide would deliver a temporary punctuation. Another psychiatric ward. This time, your roommate was a desolately lonely old woman. Her wish list begged for washing powder, and some shortbread biscuits. What role models. Your potential future stared you in the face. Institutionalized individuals happy to have slippers, deadened to a routine of art therapy. Urine-stained carpets rotting in desperation, and the smell of industrially cooked pasta languishing in plates. How could I keep you hopeful? And yet you kept trying. You kept wanting to talk. No therapy, no compassion, and then you numbed your desire by taking more illegal drugs.

The cocktail of legitimate and illegitimate medicine delivered seizures. The first one of these began as you greeted me in a hug. Your muscles went rigid, and your arms locked themselves into an embrace round my neck. I felt sad, frightened of what had happened to you. I called out to the nurses who, under-resourced, looked as vacant as the patients. The seizure electrified your muscles, contorting them into rigid postures. Your neck felt stretched in agony. Your eyes rolled up, and your jaw locked into a permanent state as if to howl with weeping. They could not get the seizures under control. Other patients urgently in need. An axe murderer had escaped the hospital grounds and was wandering the streets. Helicopters chopped the air while police and dogs sought out the bushes. Even in the middle of your contortions, they searched your room while you lay conscious but trapped in a body. Your groans a testimony to your agony on the floor. Six hours in this state. I wished all those who so effortlessly dismissed children like you could be there to witness your courage. I wished they could be there seeing how the emergency doctor on call arrived six hours later, to deliver her verdict of "oblivion".

She didn't know what had reduced you to looking like an over-stretched turkey. The ambulance arrived and we began another round in casualty. Drips and heart monitoring machines. Even in this desperate state, you worried about being touched, and sought privacy in the curtains being drawn. Your oddly coloured socks with their childish designs popped their tiny identities from beneath the hospital blankets. We so needed to be reminded you were only a child. Eventually, twelve hours later, your body rested but no hospital would offer you a bed. Managers argued about budgets and local authority funding boundaries. Eventually the high security ward of a local hospital took you again. It felt like a cruel joke.

A month later, the adults finally conceded that you should be on the children's ward. The professionals gathered their goodwill and humanity, well protected by professional veneers. I wanted to be angry, but I felt compassion. How can they work in conditions like this? So under-resourced. Their wards full of individuals with entrenched damage due to poverty and childhood neglect. The last stop for all society's ill. The holding place of human beings who the care structure was too paralyzed to help. They knew their hospital ward was no place of healing. They admitted that to get control of the illicit drugs being trafficked, they had had to stop visitors for a while. They admitted that you had had no therapy, and that you were not in the right place. Their concern was palpable, but so was their sense of defeat. Foot soldiers in an army driven by faceless generals, allowing the destruction of so many souls. The healers, like the patients, had spiritually been murdered.

What a redemption? Like a mini revolutionary I was protesting. I must've looked like some out of place nightmare. What page of the diagnostic manual would hold my label? Was I manic, or desperate not to collude with madness. They looked at me with exhaustion and dislike. Was it not enough that they felt powerless? Did I really need to reflect back at them the passion they so yearned for but had allowed to die. One of us had to be bad, for the good in the others to be preserved. I carried the pathology, because I was outnumbered. My passion for your well-being smacked of boundarylessness. In their eyes, I was too involved. It was evident in my face, in my voice, in my refusal to engage with that deadly collusive silence. I was an impostor in this professional decorum. They delivered platitudes in the hope that I would be silenced: "She is lucky to have you advocating on her behalf". Lucky? I was desperate. I was desperate not to lose you to some deadly soul factory where the diagnostic manual did the thinking. I was desperate to remind them you were only a child. So often the abuse you experienced mirrored itself in a repeat. The discourse of victim and perpetrator played itself like a relentless legacy. It seemed inescapable.

The little ward sister from the children's ward of a psychiatric hospital seemed to promise a resolution out of this vicious cycle. I wanted to believe her. I wanted the promise of art therapy, music therapy, education activities and psychotherapy. I wanted all these things for you in the kindness of the children's ward, where you could disclose your horrific secrets and feel contained and safe. I wanted psychiatrists who understood the complex intricacies of your communications, who would see you as I saw you, as a child defended in her torment, hardened not to be damaged further, and fiercely protective of the residue of feelings left in you. I wanted the doctor to meet you, human to human, mind to mind, and leave the diagnostic manual behind. But the sister looked too small, and I suspected faced with your murderous fury, she would not survive.

The first night they expressed anxiety, by the next they had made you a day patient. Your behaviour was too difficult to manage in the evenings. You had clung on to hope and your little timetable. For a short while you looked like a school child on her way to school. But yet again, they forgot the child in you, and the demonic feelings you expressed gave priority to their own needs for childlike survival. They were going to save themselves first, these grown men and women endowed with the best that science and training can afford. They gathered in a room, all fifteen of them, and I sat there in disbelief as they recounted how during your therapy session you had stood up, mid-disclosure of abuse, and declared that you would kill the perpetrators with a gun. This they perceived as too big a threat to their safety. They believed you were capable of carrying out your threat, and they were frightened. Yet again the professionals protected themselves, and let you lose to the mercilessness of the streets.

I was speechless, shocked at how they could not see the appropriateness of your rage. If they had known that during your abuse your father used weapons, they would have understood the retribution you must have fantasized as you were being overpowered by your abusers. How could they not see that the therapy and the disclosure must have felt for a moment like the indignity of being totally exposed was repeating itself? Could they not allow you your need to seek a redress in the balance of power? You had no gun in your hand. Why didn't they admit to their lack of courage?

I knew what you must've looked like. A possessed and cornered creature; like a suicide bomber, ready to die. And yet, you had been prepared to risk the disclosure. The child in you placed trust in the hands of the therapist. What betrayal to eject you from this potentially healing space. I am angry on your behalf, shocked at the lack of spiritual discipline in my colleagues. I felt sarcastic in response to their stupidity. How could they not see that the terror of the child had transferred itself onto them? They were now like you, experiencing fear, a murderous assault on their survival. Yet they were grown-ups. Where had they been when you were a child alone in your father's bleak room, overpowered by physical horrors, distorted by psychological terrors? Where were they? One betrayal of power you could forgive, but how were you to comprehend this rejection? The entire professional face of the children's psychiatric services deemed you too dangerous to treat.

They sent you a goodbye card signed by all of them. You clutched it with gratitude. I marvelled at your forgiveness, your ability to understand their position. I attempted to share your appreciation, but I was painfully aware of my own despair. I was angry, and to this day, I carry feelings of contempt because of how you were treated. We never seemed to be able to find the right therapeutic space. The initial placement in a children's semi-secure centre in the country was repeating the cycle of abuse. Every day you were overpowered by the workers in a restraint and eventually you ended up in court for assault on a member of staff. Despite being a placement for some of the most damaged children, the staff were paid only five pounds an hour. There was no therapist available, and they received no therapeutic supervision. Neither were they therapeutically trained. They had provided you with a key worker, whose behaviour was completely inappropriate. Sometimes she rang me clearly drunk, dripping with self-pity, giving accounts of her own damaged childhood. The staff comforted themselves by withholding privileges of pizza, or trips down to the local pub to play pool. For this therapeutic joke we paid £3500 a week. Half a year later the service was shut down. Every day you pleaded to be removed and eventually you drove the situation to its resolution through the only means available to you. Violence, which they could not tolerate. You ran away on the trains. Some kind train driver, despite no training, managed to calm you down in his driver's cabin, by simply sharing his humanity with you. The simplest solutions sometimes evade so many of us because we look for expertise greater than our loving intuition.

I made that mistake too. I kept looking for an institution which would eventually be the answer to your pain, not knowing that perhaps the healing process was taking place in the space made by the care shared between the two of us. I as your therapeutic caregiver, and you as the child who had placed her trust in me. I was burdened by the privilege, unsure of my resources. I so wanted the best for you even if that meant your being away from me. I kept checking my own interventions but I always knew that I was completely committed to your well-being. Who did I think was going to make the emotional sacrifice needed to pull you away from your deadly desires?

Crack was devastating your life. You had embraced this sinister murder; it was slowly killing you. Behind closed doors of private houses, groups were engaged in chasing air through the silver foil crowned bottles. The promises of clean water, advertised in beautiful sea-scaped adverts, were now servicing bleak psychological funerals. Men, women, children, gathered round crack pipes, selling their bodies when the possessions ran out. For you it was a bitter irony. Sexually abused. Too ashamed to have your flesh revealed on a hospital bed. The perversion protected you against the pain. You believed yourself master of the ceremony. You decided and you revelled in your new-found power; to earn, to control, to master, to reduce grown men into obedience.

The world seemed to have finally afforded you the power you so desperately sought. You believed yourself to be a "gangster" moving with the worst of them. You prided yourself on being able to call upon these men as backup when an injustice was done against you. You sat and watched their multi-million pound deals and rode in their cars as the girlfriend of normality, helping to disguise their business dealings behind a mask of domesticity. The mother and father of all perversions. The daddy was still abusing you little girl, but this time he gave you room to imagine yourself as the initiator. The drugs had killed your thinking, but despite this you held on to shreds of decency, and through the chinks you could see how destruction was winning.

We tried a rehabilitation programme for addicts. Even though they helped you with your flashbacks through trauma therapy, the professionals at the programme rejected you because of your anger, too. Several times, you were excluded. Desperate for help you pleaded your way back in, but they were careless, bloated with the need to earn money. Another £5000 a week, and they too thought you too difficult to treat. The doors of repair were all slamming in your face. You had reached new levels of desperation. You kept telling me prison was the only answer and you kept behaving more dangerously, so that the police would arrest you. I called them on many occasions when you hit another member of staff, and finally when, for the first time, you hit me. The police had no solution either. They told me it was a domestic assault, and it could not legally be taken up. You oscillated between hate and desperation for me, and I felt I had to set the limit at your hitting me.

Despite the rage I still remembered your littleness. I remembered you were still a child, and I was clear that giving up on you was not an option. I could not get the help you needed. When I called your psychiatrist he kept telling me how their psychiatric wards were too full and were unsuitable for you. No provision could cope with your capacity for violence, and those which could were no longer accessible to you. We had had a window of opportunity before your sixteenth birthday. The possibility of a secure unit with therapeutic help, but

neither health nor social services would pay for it. The closest you got
to a provision was one afternoon in a private adolescent hospital,
pristine and welcoming. But you were asked to pick up your bags and
return to London, because a bed had become available in South
London. Sometimes it looked like a game of musical psychiatric beds,
as managers changed their minds and debated.

Desperate to help you, we hired a cottage in the country. When I
told your psychiatrist I would take you away for detox, he looked at
me marvelling in disbelief. I could see he admired my resolve, but it
was beyond his comprehension. When we arrived in the middle of
leafy farmlands into a dreamlike cottage, you ran to claim the kitchen
knives, but your decency allowed me to take them off you and I hid
them away in the forest nearby. You, Chloe and I would travel the
depths of your despair in that week. Considering how many tranquil-
lizers rehabs use for withdrawal, I felt us brave as we battled your
addictions with herbal relaxants and faith. Chloe took you go-carting
and every minute we filled up your time with activities. At night you
lay near me, shivering uncontrollably, as the withdrawal tightened its
horrific grip. You cried that desperate cry for hours, relentlessly, as we
sat comforting you. You broke the cups and saucers seeking sharp
edges to release rivers on your arms. Five days later, you were clean and
I walked away with what I considered to be the proudest achievement
of my life. Two children's charities later, numerous degrees and accolades… being with you in that cottage surpassed them all.

Social services insisted you came back to South London and
stayed in a bed and breakfast at a local Clapham hotel. Within days
you were back on crack, as the mother of one of your friends encouraged you to take it again. What woman with a child would wish such
destruction on another? I was so disappointed and angry. I had
warned social services that this would happen, and the sickening
events unfolded. The crack was gripping. Your desire to acquire it put
you more and more at risk. Every day you felt more desperate than the
next, as dealers threatened you with death. In your worst moments
you were still profoundly honest. With tremendous courage, you
admitted to the damage you were experiencing as well as that which

you were causing. Always, you hoped, we would together find a way out.

The telephone call I had always dreaded finally arrived in the middle of the night, and then I met you in a park, you crying like a baby.

It was ugly. Shoddy. The police interviewer well rehearsed in the process of mimicking compassion. But clearly she had seen too many of these situations and had to disengage. You courageously gave them details, but they could not guarantee your protection.

The interviewer tried not to re-traumatize you with her questions. But with every word repeating the dreaded events, you shook, your tearfulness rendering you breathless. The police could not keep you safe. If they arrested the drug dealers, their associates would have come looking for you in revenge. You knew the violence these men could resort to. You had watched as they had punctured their client's kidneys, split open their skulls, because of some minor unpaid debt. What fury could have awaited you if you had revealed their address?

I felt worried and kept in touch with the police, who reluctantly let this crime go like many others, paralyzed by the supremacy of street violence. They knew they could not keep you safe, and perhaps they knew the street would deliver its own retribution.

You now could not bear to be touched. Together, we talked every day, as you agreed gently to risk some physical contact again. Your first tentative step at a beauty salon. I sat in the waiting area, as you allowed the therapist to touch your face. When you finished the session, you felt elated at being able to overcome this barrier of terror. You felt proud of being able to grow your nails, not chew them into oblivion. The next experience of touch you permitted was when we went back to the beauty salon again for you to have a manicure. Through a shade of nail varnish, the rehearsal to risk being a girl was facilitated. I so admired your resolve. Your refusal to be defeated. I had realized that perhaps the attachment you felt for me was the best way to ameliorate your self-destruction. Together, using a mobile phone and face-to-face contact, we worked to diminish your substance abuse. You stopped the crack use, the cannabis and excessive alcohol consumption. After each achievement, you felt proud of your gains. Once or twice you slipped, but regained the ground, determined to beat your addictions. The struggle to remain drug-free continues.

Your emotional and physiological thermostat was still impaired. You exploded, became upset; but instead of lashing out at others, you would remove yourself before a capacity for harm had taken over. You stopped self-harming and the scars on your arms began to fade. They reminded you of your shame.

Your new sense of calm allowed you to go to lessons. You had always wanted to read and write but schools kept permanently excluding you for bad behaviour. Your statement of special needs had not identified your specific learning difficulties. One school report claimed you could read and write two years ahead of your age. When we first met you, you couldn't form a single letter. You could not write your name, neither could you write numbers. Now you pride yourself on being able to read the *Sun* newspaper, and you write little letters, struggling to join your handwriting into a mature presentation.

The road ahead remains tough. The council has given you your own flat, a dilapidated shell, which we had to decorate and repair. Why do they do this to young people in care? They admit the state to be your parent. But where are they when you need to plaster the wall? Connect the electricity meter? How do you run a home when you have no sense of a homemaker within?

You still wanted your mother and your love was burning a hole of self-hate. But you have stopped begging her to let you be her baby. The yearning is there, but you realize her maternity is sometimes toxic, poisoned with her unresolved pain. You have so much talent, so much resolve. You are brave, and breathlessly dignified in your struggle to recover. Mindlessly your parents trampled over your childhood. Their failure to honour the task of protecting you, compounded by all those professionals who should have picked up the broken pieces. The crack a testimony to deep wounds, lines of betrayal etched into the fabric of your being.

Despite all this harm you remain beautiful, spirited and funny. I don't know what future rests ahead of you, but I know every day you will have to re-find your will to live. I apologize for all the wrongs done to you. So many of us have failed, fallen short. Chosen our well-being above yours. I apologize for the destruction of your child-hood, for the unfair burden of guilt, disgust and terror you carry within. I respect you for your courage, and I feel humbled by your capacity for hope. I hope suicide will remain only a shadow.

When this letter was read to you for your approval, you sat there motionless, the tears shading your cheeks. When I finished you were silent and then you took my pen. You wrote "I love you" in joined-up handwriting on my hand. I wished your mother was there to accept this honour. In the meantime I hold it dear in my heart while the letters fade.

PLEA FOR WISDOM

When we choose to be a therapeutic worker, we must understand the need for spiritual discipline. Healing is not found in emotional coldness. Intellect is diminished if it is divorced from the capacity to feel.

Counter transference as a diagnostic tool

Sometimes the client invokes overwhelming feelings in the worker. If you ever want to escape this experience, stand still instead, to observe the learning. The feelings transferred onto you hold information which can inform your interventions.

Behind every piece of behaviour is an intelligence awaiting decoding. Psychiatric labels do not provide us with an answer and must never be used to shield us from the clients' humanity. Clients with disturbances are no different to us. They have simply been pushed to extremes of feeling which we have been lucky not to have had forced upon us.

Disclosure of sexual abuse and aftermath

Those who have been overpowered, humiliated and abused experience catastrophic loss of power. They will seek redress, sometimes by rendering others similarly powerless. They align themselves with the powerful perpetrator, in order never to be victimized again. Don't pass judgment. In shaming them, you humiliate them further, repeating the cycle of abuse. Remind them of their capacity for goodness. Empower them through demonstrating quality of behaviour and interaction, so that they can let go of the negative behaviour.

In the client's recounting of experiences of abuse, it can feel to the client as though a therapeutic worker is holding on to power in the face of the client's powerlessness. The client may feel shame as the worker becomes an uninvolved observer. The un-abused observing the abused in a frenzied state. For the client, this can translate within seconds into a dynamic of perpetrator and victim. The therapeutic worker must align themselves with the client by gently interpreting the client's experience. However, when interpreting, be wary of creating more humiliation. Acknowledge the client's strengths in surviving rather than just their powerlessness in relation to the abusive events.

The client may need to hold on to an exaggerated sense of power, as a denial of their immense humiliation. You could acknowledge their capacity for revenge, but also their choice not to act on it. In this way, you render them powerful by pointing out their not resorting to any further harm.

Clients who have been sexually abused may overcome their fearfulness of sexual contact by taking control of sexual encounters so that within them, they retain supreme power. The client may mirror the abusers' behaviour, by adopting the role of a sexual predator. Sometimes the same client may be repulsed and refuse sexual contact and be terrified of it. There is often a vacillation between being perversely attracted to sexually inappropriate situations and being repulsed by any form of sexuality.

If the client senses that the therapeutic workers wish for their sexual re-engagement, they may experience this intervention as further manifestations of abuse, as if the worker is now like a perpetrator pressurizing them into unwanted sexual contact.

Sometimes clients re-enact elements of the abuse within the therapeutic relationship. They may torment the worker, very much like the abusers tormented them. Rather than being defensive, gently acknowledge that in making you vulnerable, they may be communicating how they felt when they were being treated badly.

You could then explore the theme and use your own feelings in order to understand what the client may have felt at that time.

For clients who have been abused, suicidal feelings may serve not just as a wish for death, but also as the last remaining sense of powerfulness. If all else has been taken away, the option of suicide remains as a reminder of some sense of agency. The capacity for control remains when all other controls have failed them.

Professional counter-transference of terror

Groups of professionals need to remain vigilant about their capacity for infantile feelings when clients overwhelm their sense of potency. Supervision will help distinguish a legitimate sense of danger from those generated by over-identification with the client's sense of being terrified.

Very distressed clients may require a therapeutic structure which has a capacity for robustness to deal with physically violent manifestations of distress. However, robustness which is not informed by compassion and delivered therapeutically risks being perceived by the client as another enactment of abuse.

In the event of having had to physically restrain a distressed client, remember to repair any potential damages to the therapeutic relationship by talking through the events which led to the restraint. In order not to shame the client, remind them of how they may not have wanted to react aggressively, but seemed unable to hold on to the good. Even if a wrong has been done, preserve the client's sense of dignity by acknowledging at least their desire for goodness, even if poor controls lead to negative behaviours.

Self-harm and its functions

Clients rarely behave randomly or illogically. They may store negative experiences from previous exchanges and call upon these to fuel revenge. Make an attempt to trace the emotional origin of an outburst rather than simply dismissing the outburst as negative.

Self-harm is at times an act of violence on the self, but sometimes clients with feelings which are too overwhelming may resort to self-harm as a means of regaining control. The experience of physical pain is deemed to be more easily identifiable and conducive to comprehension than emotional pain.

Clients may feel too ashamed to cry; they may experience crying as defeat. They may feel powerless and humiliated when crying in the presence of the worker. They may perceive the worker as having too much power over them. When crying is too difficult, the release of blood through self-harm can be perceived as a substitute for tears. Some research shows self-harm to have a cycle of tension buildup and then release, mirrored by the sudden availability of endorphins (calming chemicals within the brain). In order to help the client, you may have to acknowledge the helpfulness of their self-harm in managing and organizing their emotions. At times, substitutes such as ice being held in the palm of their hands may act as an intermediary before they are able to abstain from self-harm behaviour altogether.

Clients may sometimes feel ashamed of the scars caused by self-harm, and sometimes proud of them. The scars may be trophies, acknowledging the client's sense of power, a reminder of the self-punishment inflicted upon herself for her self-disgust.

Self-harm can be addictive and function as an avoidance of complex feelings. Self-harm can be a substitute for speech, telling the worker of the magnitude of the client's pain, a visible testimony to their torment. Self-harm done in front of the therapeutic worker can be a means by which the client makes the therapist experience herself as powerless in relation to the abuse being perpetrated. The client in self-harming becomes a perpetrator in relation to herself. The therapist, like the client, experiences impotence, unable to prevent the abuse. Instead of telling clients to stop self-harming, explore the function of it in the client's psychological constellation.

Lack of maternal care issues

Clients who have experienced maternal deprivation have complex attitudes towards caregivers. On the one hand, they yearn for maternal care and they elicit it in the caregiver. On the other hand, when you show them care they may feel humiliated. The feeling of humiliation is often generated when the therapeutic worker draws attention to the presence of a baby–mother interaction within the relationship. Clients may rebuff this observation because they feel too unworthy of being someone's baby. If their own mothers didn't want them, then they must be too bad for a substitute maternal experience to allow them that baby space. Clients may also have survived by denying any need for maternal love, so your reminding them of their baby needs may feel like an attack on their sense of power.

A client may elicit maternal care in the therapeutic worker by exaggerating their experiences of maternal deprivation. They may also maintain their loyalty to their mother by hiding from her their attachment to the therapeutic worker. In order to make their own mother care more, the client may present the therapeutic worker as abusive. This is a test. Will their own mother come to the rescue? Or will she be, yet again, neglecting? The same pattern may be repeated in reverse. The client may test how much the therapist cares by recounting their mother's failings to generate rescuing behaviours in the therapist.

All these distortions in communication are manifestations of maternal deprivation. A client who needs to exaggerate the harm she has experienced is a client who feels desolate, empty and emotionally unfed. Take care not to humiliate the client by naming the game. Simply acknowledge that you understand how much she misses the experience of being mothered, and how well she has survived despite the absence.

In experiencing a potential loss of power, abused clients often feel at risk of being abused again. They may experience any interpretation, or the acknowledgement of their diminished power, as a repeat of the persecutor–persecuted relationship.

Physical outcomes of emotional trauma

Clients exposed to relentless trauma may experience a physiological breakdown, impacting their immune and digestive systems. An interplay between adrenalin and noradrenalin (the flight–fright hormones) as well as cortisol (the stress hormone), creates a complex chemistry, both battling with and generating stress. The hyper-distressed client is quick to explode and takes much longer to calm down from an outburst. For these clients a more holistic intervention may be necessary.

Clients who experience physical illness or distress may perceive these conditions as their bodies behaving in an out-of-control way. They may experience their bodies as either an abuser or being abused. Any physical manifestations of distress must be explored in relation to their meaning in terms of the original experiences of trauma. But at the same time clients must not be accused of becoming ill because of the abuse they have experienced as this may feel like an insult to their sense of agency and control.

CHAPTER 4

Shame

Letter to Daisy

DEAR DAISY,

Today the A-level results came out. They were fantastic. We did not expect anything less. I felt so proud of your achievement, and the image of you as a ten-year-old flashed in front of my eyes. You always had a perfectly clean white school shirt, immaculately ironed. An energetic little girl, intelligent and curious, you were bullied at your primary school and I could never understand why your secondary school kept excluding you. You spent long days off school, wandering the streets.

I asked for permission to visit your home. Nothing could have prepared me for the shock. I could barely make my way up the stairs. Your little room, desperate, without furniture. You slept on the floor. Your clothes in dustbin liners. I suddenly understood the meaning behind the perfect white shirt. The extraordinary dignity you always maintained in the face of all challenges. It wasn't about poverty because your mother worked the night shift. Your stepfather looked after his little boy, but he did not live at home. Every room in this house was devastated. There was no order. The kitchen rejected its food. Piles of frying pans, drowned with their burns, soot bleak, black and dirty green grey. There was no room. Even in the garden the greenness of the grass was attacked by discarded and damaged furniture. It was soulless, the house. A child factory unsympathetic to its children. Your mother sat in the armchair, full of indignation at how you failed to meet her needs. I felt angry at her mental pollution. You were only a little girl. How could she leave you to such dirt and bleakness? The bathroom was too burdened with grime to offer any resolution. I felt speechless and moved to tears by your aspiration to quality. How had you managed to hold on to a sense of excellence in the middle of so much mindless mess? I tried talking to your mother about cleaning up the house, offered to help, but she saw it as your responsibility. You the little ten-year-old with your single white shirt. I knew every night you must have washed it and ironed it to escape indignity in the morning.

Your oldest brother was imprisoned for drugs and violent crimes. The second eldest is also in prison. He had so wanted to be "legit" but his resolve failed and at sixteen he was incarcerated. Both of you fatherless, born to an unknown man. Your mother too preoccupied with her own needs to acknowledge yours.

One of your sisters worked at the bank. She too was intelligent, but her soul seemed defeated as if she was too tired to protest. She'd given up on your mother as maternal carer, and instead serviced her needs as best as she could to buy peace. Your older sister, in contrast, was full of protest. She pulled the water pipes off the walls, furious, as if speech could no longer have any impact. Social services had removed her from the family home, and the despair eventually manifested itself in a schizophrenic breakdown. Despite the breakdown, she had more maternal capacity than your mother. Sometimes she would buy you a gift, and often she would protest at your mother's inability to care for you, her refusal to take responsibility for your childhood.

One day, the fire brigade rang. Your little legs were dangling off the window ledge. You were refusing to move. They asked for my help to talk you down. The officers were afraid you might jump to your death, but you were not defeated, you were not frightened. You were holding all of them to ransom, communicating your protest, and demanding justice in the face of your mother's manipulation. She was so good at presenting herself as victim when she perpetrated the greatest assaults on your childhood. She hit you, never cooked, left you all night alone in the house. By morning she would turn up at your school, ready to renounce you as her daughter. Did she admit to the shit-hole she had condemned you to? To the perversion of care she had exposed you to? Would the head teacher realize your mother was the abuser, not you? Would they see through her self-justification, her eloquent complaints about how horrible you were to her?

I was so angry. Social services had left you and your siblings, one of them only six years old, in these conditions. They never visited to check on your welfare, when they had seen the disturbed conditions you all lived in. Your bad behaviour was an excuse. You were seen as the embodiment of the family's ills. The social worker who eventually visited, forced by the school, colluded with the family's view, thinking she would cajole you into submission and make you like your bank clerk sister, silently passive, defeated and too weary to survive. You became more and more defiant, more angry at the injustice. Sometimes the rage would feel too much and you would lose your control in a furious expulsion. Beng, one of our staff, held you in a gentle restraint. You spat at him and kicked him, for all the missed fathers in your life. You battered him for all the wrongs done to you, and yet he stood containing your fragmentation in a kind embrace.

Your own terror terrified you. Shocked to see so much feeling expressed, you changed and as time went on your fight became less expressive. Not for you, the scream of pain. Instead, you developed a steely resolve. The heat of your anger turned ice sharp, razor vigilant for any betrayal. You watched those of us who showed you care and punished us with your cold rejection when we failed to honour your need. We had to step like delicate ballerinas on your fragile stage. Even though you had acquired more control, I felt your pain, your littleness, your fierce protection of your dignity. What greater shame than rejection by a mother? Her public and vocal denunciation of her daughter. Every teacher watched as she berated you, and finally banished you from the family home. You were only fourteen years old. Only a child. In order to save money, social services placed you with your schizophrenic sister. Two needy children living together, and yet there was so much courage in both your resolves to make a home.

We bought you a bed, and some furniture. We helped you with your practical needs, and from a distance lovingly watched out for your welfare. The headteacher was the first to acknowledge the truth. She recognized the drama of your life originated in the abuse and neglect perpetrated by your mother. She offered the school washing machine for you to wash your clothes.

You kept going like a valiant soldier, never complaining. But you were so so emotionally delicate. You refused any help, which would risk exposing your vulnerability. Often friends would promise to be there for you, and then their teenage fickleness would feel like a bleak betrayal. You never protested, because to object would require you to admit need and you couldn't afford to do so. To need felt shameful. You were always so afraid of a potential rejection. How could you be sure that we would care for you without resentment when your own mother had objected to your childlike need? Sometimes I wondered if you thought yourself worthy of any love.

Your basic struggle to survive, and the challenges it threw up, never culminated in a psychological crisis. The relative calm of your sister's house gave way to her schizophrenic frenzy. Once you came home to find your clothes cut to shreds by your brother, who during an argument had accused you of stealing from his room. Such an attack on the precious possessions you had accumulated. Your clothes were your currency of dignity; dressed in your designer wear you experienced equality. No one knew from what poverty and struggle you had emerged. We laughed at your stylishness, marvelled at your sense of glamour, you could have easily been peeled off the pages of *Vogue*, and now one of the people closest to you had devastated the illusion. I felt your hurt, but you would not allow me the verbalization, as if the admission would be the final blow, and your fragile sense of self would collapse with defeat.

Your sister was sectioned under the Mental Health Act at a local hospital. At first, you tried to visit her, but the image of her as fragmented, small and shattered was too unbearable. You were afraid of the other patients, afraid of the desolation reflected back at you. Your resolve to be strong became even more entrenched. You refused to visit. She had no other visitors. Some might have thought you cruel, but it was a choice necessary for your survival. If you broke down, you did not believe anyone would be there to pick up the pieces. I knew you were hurting. I saw it in your eyes when you let yourself weep for another child who was losing it in a frenzied act of despair. You saw how devastated the other child was, and in that devastation you were, potentially, reflected back. You still a fourteen-year-old little girl with your white school shirt, perfectly ironed. Inside, you must have suppressed fountains of weeping.

For a while you kept going alone in that house. Social services sold your childhood to their thresholds, too snowed under with demands, they left you to manage on your own, as you always had done. Alone and like a dignified soldier walking through an unrelenting landscape. I cried for you, but dared not show my tears. You were so tentatively glued together. Your sister's rage magnified, maybe she wanted you to break, your intactness an affront to her sense of survival. What destructive envy drove her to seek your paralysis? To lock you out of her house in the middle of your GCSE exams? You were homeless, you were back to the bin liner holding your worldly possessions.

We pleaded with social services to find you accommodation. They refused. You were soon not to be deemed legally a child. At sixteen, they could write you out of their books. You were yet another name soon to disappear off the responsibility roster. I was shocked. What civilized society treats its vulnerable children like this, and then pleads the cause of the starving in Africa? This spiritual famine in the local authority social services was more rotten, more repugnant. We placed you in a local hotel. The manager and cleaning ladies kept an eye on you while you slept there. Every night you closed the door, taking your isolation to bed. Who was there to encourage you? To console you and provide you with milk and kindness as you negotiated one of the biggest milestones of your life?

Some teachers criticized your precocious independence, your fierce no-nonsense sensibilities. But were they there in that hotel room, to know that even if you had cried the white sheets could do no more than absorb your tears in the silence? Social services waited, leaving you homeless. If we hadn't been there, you would have had your sitting room on the streets. When you reached sixteen, the housing department inherited you. A cold bureaucracy showing you maps of where you could potentially live, and then placing you in dangerous and unsupervised hostels. The showers wept dirt. The hostels were places of risk, with drug dealing adolescents stabbing and shooting each other to avenge a debt, and girls who despised you for what they perceived to be your "classiness". Next door, men having sex with young vulnerable girls. You despaired at how you would hold on to your sense of excellence in the midst of such sleaziness.

Eventually a safer hostel was found, but you were smarter than the hostel workers, who resented your style and wanted you crushed. You were thought to be above your station. Everybody stood by, waiting to see you fall off the pinnacle of excellence you had set yourself. In between, you collected your pennies to make it to the school ski trip. You worked weekends in clothes shops. Your efforts, always an inspiration. Your intelligence breathtaking.

Your GCSE results delivered many A and B grades. I knew how much resolve and courage it had taken. As you achieved in academic terms, your fragility challenged your control. You noticed pain in others. You felt indignant on behalf of school friends who were being neglected, but you never complained about your own deprivation. You would stand in front of business leaders giving a speech explaining the plight of young people on benefits. They admired your astuteness, your composure, your political know-how, but they did not know the little girl with a single white school shirt. They did not know tonight you would walk past drug dealers in the street shadows, and turn the key to your hostel door.

On your eighteenth birthday, one of the most special days of a child's life, you only received a card from your brother in prison. The other gifts were from mentors we had provided for you. One of them was so sensitive to your needs, so aware of your delicate control. No word from your mother. She had forgotten your childhood, and now that you entered the adult world she didn't celebrate either. She never came to visit you, to find out how her child was doing. When the A-level results came out, she never rang to inquire. You didn't ask for anything from her, but I often wondered about what her rejection was doing to you.

At eighteen, the housing department offered you your own flat, but you had no one to help you move in. Your entire life was packed into a small cardboard box, and yet you decorated your flat like a designer, only acquiring the best. I wanted you to consider second-hand furniture, but for you this meant Shame. What worried me was your tremendous upset. I worried about how much energy you used up, keeping yourself together. So much courage had an inevitable cost. I knew you battled against your own emotional desolation. I got glimpses of it when you had to do your essays. It felt like the homework was too great a demand. You rested your little head on your arms, battling away the tears. You experienced any work which felt too challenging like an unbearable assault on your sense of dignity. Often you were profoundly tired. The burden of having to take sole responsibility for your own survival at such a young age so unjust.

Sometimes you were so busy keeping yourself respected that you unwittingly disrespected others. Your manner, at times, appeared arrogant and aloof. People sometimes felt dismissed by your seeming disdain. You had little mercy for those less intelligent, except if they were socially and emotionally vulnerable. You presented with such paradoxes. Empathic and kind. Rejecting and seemingly unapprecia- tive. You struggled to remember to thank people. I understood you could not afford to admit to other people's importance in your life. What if they too rejected you? If you had acknowledged your need for others then you would also have had to worry about the absence of someone you could really rely on.

I was worried. Your resolve to survive your loneliness was pushing people away from you and sustaining the isolation. I wanted to explain that your friends didn't turn up to help because they believed you didn't need them. But even my observations felt close to a state- ment of your potential worthlessness. I could not discuss any short- comings in case you perceived me as not liking you, like your mother.

You kept some friends, but I also watched people reject you by simply walking away. They were trying non-contention to spare both of you the humiliation. You were so honourable. You wanted no gifts because you felt it meant you had to return the favour, and you couldn't afford to do so, in either emotional or practical terms. As you refused good gifts, however, the perverse gifts took over. You deliv- ered revenge for the rejection and received rejection in exchange.

People felt useless the more you denied needing them. They often forgot how little you were and believed your independence beyond the illusion. When people gave to you both practically and emotionally, you needed to deny it so that you wouldn't be bound to them in the return of the favour. You couldn't admit the need and neither did you have the resources to give of yourself.

Your sense of shame was so profound. You were afraid to give to others, in case your offering insulted their sense of dignity. Equally people felt afraid to give to you, in case their contribution fell short of your standards and resulted in your believing the gesture to reflect your worthlessness. The fear and responsibility of receiving so profoundly separated you from others. It is as if your shame at being rejected by your mother condemned you to rejecting others and in turn being rejected. It wasn't because you welcomed loneliness. It was because you needed safety – safety from the devastations of humiliation. You could not make the onlookers blind. Instead, you absented yourself.

I worried about your capacity for relationships. I wanted to make sure your boyfriend understood that beneath the sophisticated façade there was a vulnerable little girl. Someone needed to take control of loving you. The vigilant space between you and others was shriveling you up, but closeness spelt terror, it felt like you could be obliterated. You couldn't give up the control, the self-scrutiny or the observation of others. You had to be in charge, because you were the only person you had.

Objects have acquired a tremendous importance in your life. They feed you, provide you with illusions of dignity. You spend a lot of time trying to acquire the right clothes, the right furniture, and the right status. You have such a need to drag yourself out of a potential ghetto. I understand this desperation you have, but I also worry about it. It's too fragile a structure on which to build the foundation of your self-esteem.

There are people you love but only from a distance. Your bank clerk sister, with her new baby. You care for your nephew. But even with your sister, the distance is maintained. I do not know what the future holds for you. I'm not sure at what point, if ever, you will be able to face your emotional vulnerability. All I know is that your courage and resolve is extraordinary. I hope that your sharp intelligence and your significant intellect will serve you well, but above all, I wish you real love, when you are strong enough to risk it. I am sorry for the damage your mother has created in your life. I am sorry that social services were negligent in their care, when they should have shielded you against your mother's assaults. I am sorry for your being a lone soldier. When I read this letter to you, tears rolled down your beautiful face and you thanked me for telling your truth.

PLEA FOR WISDOM

The impact of shame and defences against it

When a child has been deprived of a parent's love, they internalize the sense of shame. They perceive it as a statement about their unworthiness. Shame is visible. Others can see it. They can see that the individual has experienced an affront to their sense of self-esteem. Shame is public, where guilt is private. In shame there is an experience of a catastrophic loss of power which others have witnessed.

Children who have had to survive on their own and meet their own needs find it difficult to ask for help. They expect others to reject them. Often the sense of isolation is so profound that the child may doubt that they even exist.

Shamed children seek redress. They climb the ladder of worth by using substitutes for love to suggest status. To regain lost self-esteem, children may align themselves with people, or goods, which may support increase in status.

Seeking enhanced status is survival behaviour. It's not psychological narcissism. Unless they are worthwhile and wanted, children who have been rejected by their parents will expect rejection from all those they come into contact with.

To discuss shameful experiences with clients requires sensitivity. It's extremely important to avoid generating further humiliation within the therapeutic encounter. Clients may need to deny their shame-inducing experiences, so as not to be humiliated further.

Children may narrow down their fields of experience to areas in which they have substantial and confirmed expertise. In this way they minimize any risk of failure and further public humiliation.

Children who have experienced shame may not be able to sustain eye contact. They may perceive other people's glance to be a means by which their lack of self-worth becomes visible. Children may be afraid that they may not be chosen because they are too bad.

Shame leading to excessive self-sufficiency

Shamed children are at times excessively self-sufficient. They do not ask for help, for fear of being turned down.

Often these children don't admit to need as they consider any need to be a failing in their self-sufficiency.

Sometimes the resolve to be self-sufficient can lead to children coming across as cold and ungrateful.

At times there is an excessive denial of other people's contributions; admitting to other people's involvement is like saying they are needed. Children who have been shamed find it difficult to admit to need.

CHAPTER 5

Adaptive Violence

Letter to Mr Mason

DEAR MR MASON,

I laughed when you told me what your pseudonym was going to be. Mr Mason. It is so you. The conspiratorial personality. How you love the secret societies, curious about their rituals and rights of membership.

Mr Mason, your speech is so layered, disguising every word. You at once suspect the person you relate to and yet deeply yearn for their caring.

You were a vulnerable fourteen-year-old when I first met you. I remember it was hard work to relate to you. You were suspicious, verbally challenging. Even your white grin glinted with the expectation you would be confronted by corruption. The paranoia could slice the air between us. I didn't know how to take your nervous laugh. I was your alleged enemy to whom you were so drawn, about whom you were so curious. Your quick and sharp wit was admirable, faster than a racing car. Before one had grasped the magnitude of the significance of your observation, another would be delivered with devastating speed.

Once I asked for your earliest memories. You described you and your mother walking down the street in Jamaica. Suddenly your

favourite dog was run over by a bus, crushed beneath the wheels. You
were two years old and you seem to remember it as if it was yesterday. I
searched for a feeling or reaction, but you gave none. Then you
described how one day, when you were aged fourteen, you and your
mother went round to the house of a man who was harassing the
family. You both robbed the house and then stabbed his dog to death.
Shock prevented me from thinking. As time has gone on, I have kept
pondering the link between your dog run over by the bus, and the dog
you both killed.

Your next memory was of when you were about four years old
with caned hair standing in the bath. The woman who was washing
you was not your mother. She was a kindly neighbour who had taken
you into her care while your mother was in prison. No arrangement
had been made by social services, neither had this woman been
checked or vetted to care for you. You suspected that like your mother
she was a drug user, but she seemed to have maintained her capacity
for loving care.

Most of your life your mother has struggled with her drug addiction. The first time I met her was when she was walking down the
street. She seemed to be so kindly, small and gentle, but she was also
like a lost child. I suddenly understood your fierce protection of her
and your compassion. She seemed frail as if she could be swept away
by the wind and blown with the leaves.

You did not remember when your mother came back from prison
but it was clearly years later. There seems to be no sense of your having
missed her and yet your love for her is so palpable. When I've talked to
you in search of your feelings about your childhood we seem to reach
an emotionally arid space.

Your clearest memories are of fighting for survival. You have
grown up not knowing if the man who claims to be your step-father is
really your father. His disowning of his son seems mindlessly cruel. At
times of need he gave you a room but charged you for it. The dislike
between the two of you is, disturbingly, taken for granted. It is as if
neither of you has chosen the other as worthy of acknowledgement.
When you were at primary school he took your sister and left the

family home. He had chosen your sister as the child to acknowledge and you as the one to deny.

Your mother acquired a job and some hope of normality, but one of her partners reported her for drug abuse and alleged dealing. She lost her employment and plunged the family into deeper poverty. You were the man of the house but only a little boy still at primary school. Your razor-lethal anger was evident already. Frequent protests or outbursts were not for you. Instead you were like a silent killer, waiting to harm your prey when they had crossed the line. You never rushed to get revenge, never chased the victims. You would wait, storing up the revenge until they arrived into your space and then you would deal them a devastating blow. You present with such extraordinary paradox. I should not like you. I should not feel safe with you. You have killed, stabbed, and yet you have such capacity for kindness, your communication is so thoughtful, your gaze so compassionate.

Your psychology escapes the simplicity of the diagnostic manual. Your crimes, your paranoid demeanour, and your capacity for cruelty could easily earn you the sociopath label, but there is so much gentleness in your exchanges with me. It is as if some living ideal has been robbed from you.

You described how your life could have been perfect. You and your mother. But your eldest sister had developed a relationship with a very disturbed man who used to batter her. In search of protection she arrived at the family home and began living there. Every day outside the doors was her crazed partner, shouting, threatening to burn you all. No injunction would keep him at bay. As he was denied access he became more crazed. It was his dog you and your mother stabbed to pieces. To escape his attention your mother left the family home and moved in with a drug addict who became your step-father. I remember you describing how you slept with knives under your pillow, forever alert to the need to defend yourself and your mother. Your step-father was violent and he violated your mother through the battering. You often lay in your bed desperate and distressed for her, and then in the end you stabbed him, punctured his kidneys and liver, delivered him to a coma but not to death. Another incident provoked you to stab him again and this time your mother insisted you left the family home. She was scared by your lethal aspirations to murder. Neither of them reported to the police or pressed charges.

By the age of twelve you were drifting from house to house, a beggar to food and care. You always felt embarrassed of having such need and yet you were alone, an urban soldier, waiting for the patience of one friend's mother to run out before you turned to another. Your days were long and mindless. Your mother had not been able to provide the bus fare for secondary school and you eventually opted out because you could not tolerate the embarrassment of being denied such basics. Your absence from school delivered you into the underbelly of the city where similarly lonely children survive on leftovers of other people's humanity.

As a group all you children were linked through tendrils of hate. Hostility kept you all motivated. You would define your territory with markings and then if another child trespassed you would punish them for the transgression. The press called you all "feral" and attributed to your loose groupings a sophisticated organization of full-blown street gangs.

The truth is more pathetic. Many of you have mothers who are drug addicts and fathers who are guests of her majesty's prisons. Often your fathers had multiple relationships and discarded the baby mothers with their babies. Your homes were unwelcoming and depleted. The wallpaper peeled itself from the walls, putrid. The chairs were marked with cigarette burns and sick. Scattered drugs paraphernalia were the household ornaments. Local takeaways provided the households food, £1.99 for greasy chicken and chips.

You all barely had any clothes, one pair of designer trainers would be your pride and joy. Although you never worried too much about showing off your goods, your subtlety disguised a gasping desperation. For twenty-one years of your life you received nothing on your birthday or Christmas from your family or friends. No one carried you in their mind, thought about your needs. I felt like crying when you told me you wished someone could have bought you a gift. Sometimes your mother would give you some money but you wanted her motherhood not her leftover coins. Yet you loved her so much, you felt for her courage, her effort to keep herself alive. Her own survival took up all her capacity. She had very little spare to give you. For you, material goods became like maternal goods, symbolizing security. As long as you had money you could maintain your frenzied self-calm. Your bit of gold, your stashed notes under the mattress, none of it earned because you had worked legitimately.

None of you could work. You were too distressed to obey a boss, unable to tolerate somebody else's power, because all power is perceived as destructive and perverse. None of you could abide by any rules, turn up on time to the monotonous setting of a fast-food outlet.

You all participated and survived through an underground economy with its own rules. As young boys of ten or eleven you sought routes out of the desperate poverty and depletion of your households. The role models strutted their wares around the estates, older boys who had made it through the drug trade. They showed you, the older ones, the peripheries of the business. The eighteen- and nineteen-year-olds ran you as couriers for the class B drugs, as older adult men ran them for the class A drugs. The system is as disciplined as any major business, yet it is perverse. If you are a young boy or girl really short of money, you can rent a phone line and work it for a couple of days. A mobile phone was at the end of it and a fictitious name, and then you could deliver the required drugs to your clientele with one call.

What made me angry is that all your clients were the same middle class, platitude-pedalling moralists who, in their radio programmes, newspapers and at their dinner parties, referred to you all as the scum of the earth. By day they would call you all feral, beastly, anti-social spongers, and by night they would run you to their houses to feed their addictions and their privilege.

The telephone lines you rented would cost £50 for the day and on a good run you would make £300 on top. People think it easy money, but the business is policed through silence and cruelty. One of your peers was assassinated at a bus stop for not paying a £70 debt to a dealer. The dealer had given him faulty drugs to carry. He broke the rules of the street by not returning the money, and in return an assassin was sent.

A poor, crack addicted, crazed young boy with a job to do at the bus stop. A stab in the neck. The blood traced the grating on the tiles of the local MacDonald's, and the boy was dead. The incident was recorded on CCTV but someone removed the tape. We held the funeral at the Arches. All of you were there. It could have been any one of you. All you boys carried his coffin. The only time you got to wear suits was on such bleak occasions. Bus loads of you we took to the funeral, you little children of this perverse trade. His street name was Sparrow, a commemoration of his sorrow.

The dealers were lethal. We struggled to reclaim you from them. One of your friends wanted to go to school again, be a child again. The dealer would not have it. He kept chasing him down, dragging him to the car from the pavement, filling his throat with the barrel of a gun. When the boy resisted, he chased him up at his house. He chased him up and down the piss bleak staircases shooting at him, wanting to kill him. Death was better than desertion.

It was much harder than working in a fast-food outlet. Every day you were all afraid. You all talked of your having been lucky that you were not dead that day. Every morning you woke up wondering if today would be your last. The adult male drug dealers sat in their leather sofas pressing the remote, like bosses of massive conglomerates. You little boys ran for them, every day dodging death and the police.

Maybe you would have risked asking for help, but how could you when you thought even the police officers were buying your drugs or re-selling what they had repossessed back on the street. So much moral and emotional corruption. Where could you find the most valuable of all emotions, where was trust?

One night on your nineteenth birthday you walked out of your house. Someone attacked you with a metal bar from behind. The blows cracked open your skull. You lost consciousness and I feared we would lose you. I visited you in the hospital. You were so little, curled up in bed, weary with pain, with living. You cried, the only time you could remember crying. Your little tiny hands with their bitten fingernails reached out to me like a toddler for the holding. One of your hands had lost all movement and feeling. You were desperate, you wanted its mobility back. Without it you could not survive on the street, it was your shooting hand. No mother to visit you in hospital, no father. The lonely urban fighter lay tiny in the hospital bed surrounded by the pound shop striped plastic zipper bags holding all your possessions. You asked me for socks and boxers. Your speech was slurred, and I was terrified at how much damage the blow had caused your brain.

It was as if the nurses knew you were relative-less. They were functional in their care, almost cold. The rejection propelled a lump in my throat. I fought back my tears as I watched you drift in and out of your nightmares, moaning. Your paranoia escalated. The nurses could not cope, too under-resourced to talk to you. I could see their sense of everything having to be done in a rush. They were driving their trolleys up and down the aisles of desperation.

I asked for a psychiatric assessment, some support for the trauma you had suffered. The psychiatrist was unavailable and the rush to give your bed away forced you prematurely out of the hospital. Where could you go? Who could care for you? Your mother and stepfather were in prison. You had no bed of your own to go to. I felt desperate in the face of your desolation.

Eventually we managed to persuade your sister to give you a room in your father's house. The cruelty of the man was breathtaking. He wanted rent. For a while you stayed there, always knowing that the only person who could give you care was yourself. In the midst of this chaos, your sister was kidnapped and held hostage in a flat. I never understood why she had become involved with such dangerous individuals. You went to rescue her and you also got trapped. They tied you both up with ropes ready to shoot you, but your ingenious survival skills shifted the embrace of the rope and you escaped through the windows, taking her with you.

It seemed relentless, the horrors being hurled at you. There seemed to be no resting place, no space for peace. Every night you moved from floor to floor. Everywhere you put your head down, danger lurked. Terrified that you might become another murder statistic we eventually found you somewhere to live. We came in and took over the care you had needed through all your childhood. We

provided you with a flat, decorated it, and for the first time in your life
you were able to have a place to call home. You were safe, and we
laughed at the routine. You enjoyed the cleanliness, the food in the
fridge, the peace; and sometimes you would ring me, the ease and
delight in your voice a true gift.

So much of your life has been about malignant violence and yet
somehow you have retained a sense of quality. Your peers were
gang-raping girls and behaving perversely. Your violence was different. It was about justice, about redressing the balance of power. You
only committed acts of violence when someone had violated you, or
someone you cared for. I wish I could say you had control, but the
outburst when it came would be automatic, almost as if programmed
like a switch.

The provocation of your violence could always be traced back to
its origin, but it triggered something catastrophic. Sometimes the girls
would reject your attention and the rejection would feel unbearable, as
if you were turning to another female like you had turned to your
mother, and like her they could not meet you halfway, at a meeting
point where both your existence could be affirmed. The girls' rejection, to you, was unjust, devastating. It risked obliterating your very
existence.

You laugh but you are lethal. When enraged you spell murder, your
body like a rapid bomb unleashes devastating blows. You describe
how you despise your victim for begging. You hate their emotional
pleading. Their vulnerability reflects back your childhood desperation, long buried, for there was no one to soothe it. You avoid shame
like the plague. Not for you, being humiliated again. Not for you,
being powerless in the grasp of the powerful. You never plead. You
were always prepared to die. Like a suicide bomber you have no life
you care to preserve.

Even today your living is like the turn of a roulette table. Maybe
prison, maybe death. Your deadliness a product of your emotional
exhaustion.

Deep down you have lost your sense of identity as a life-seeking
force. You gave up your will to live to the nights you trembled with
terror, to the long days waiting for your mother to be released from

prison. Maybe too many times your mother looked like she was dying, drugged, battered, donating her teeth to crack cocaine. Maybe all these things have severed your link with living. Sometimes I sense your desperate yearning, your thirst for security. You seek me out to review the list of your lifelines, your reasons to keep alive, but they are always material things – a car, some money, some gold, a house.

The women, you hate but pity; the men deserve no mercy if they consider themselves superior to you. No more being a powerless victim witnessing the death of those you love. Your dog died, your mother shut down her shutters of care chasing druggie smokes down alleyways. Your father denied your identity. Never again will they trample your existence. Your lethal potential can be unleashed with a disturbed minute's notice. They killed you, so you can kill.

If I could teach you grieving maybe we could retrieve your feelings, return you to the living, but where will I find you somewhere safe for the healing of your weeping? You keep telling me it will be prison. The only predictable resting place for those too exhausted to kill themselves. Those who aspire to suicide are still attempting a form of reparation, a release from suffering, albeit perverse, but Mr Mason you don't have enough will to fix nothing. You can drift for days on end like a walking dead person.

As I write this letter to you a moth is hurling itself mindlessly at the wall. Sometimes you make me feel that way. I do not know where to begin. The damage seems so profound, your walls so impregnable, and yet some childlike yearning keeps both of us meeting. I sense your potential, your compassion. I understand your murderous retrievals of justice. I want to help return your identity to you. I want to reflect your goodness back at you. I want to help rekindle your love of learning. You are so intelligent. Your paranoia is unfulfilled thinking. You imagine the listener; the intellectual adversary has become an imagined enemy. How can I tell you this when you have battled so many real threats to your life? So many savage attacks on your attachments. How can I make you believe in the safeness of being alive?

Together we sit on a bench and plan your future – how you will go to college, make money out of a legitimate business, have a stable family with no hostages to addiction. As we dream your courage has been fortified. Now you stand within a group, without each member feeling like a threat to your very existence. Now you can imagine going to college, the prospectus is on your table at home. Now you can travel without believing every male to be an undercover police officer following you around. Your world view is stilling itself, the threats are subsiding, and then maybe you can risk loving again and in the energy of it feel alive.

As I write this letter your mother and step-father are in prison again. He alleges she not only consumed class A drugs but also dealt in them. You cannot believe his betrayal. The judges were accepting her vulnerability as an addict, why add to her crimes in this way? Your rage was intense. Even in the courtroom, he abused her. This time your mother's sentence increased to five years. You go to visit her, take her a pair of trainers and a music CD. You worry for her well-being, so tender, but the sadness of it drags my heart. It should be her visiting you.

You recently escaped prison after half a year on remand – allegedly you shot a man and a boy with multiple bullets. I don't know if it is true, but I know you are capable of it, once your rage triggers have been unleashed. You are always shocked by your own reactions. You want help not to be so lethal. Above all you want normality.

People will sit in judgement of your capacity for violence, but they do not realize that you and similarly brutalized children are appropriate products of your environments. Poor attachment relationships and neglect, early violations of your sense of safety, deprivation of love all conspire to deliver an inner deadness and deadliness. In the willingness to die, the will to kill finds an environmentally relevant expression. You all look out of your windows and the learning is there. At first as children you are robbed and "juked" (stabbed in the leg or arm) by older teenagers. These attacks harden your resolve to hate and the seeking of revenge. The experience of being attacked and no one being held accountable gives you a world view empty of legitimate justice.

There are no resources to fund enough police. Crime is a normality, violation of personal space the normal social currency of the inner city. The absence of safety creates an alternative system of justice. For families with fathers and uncles, transgressions are redressed by the relatives distributing justice. It is a sickly fair game. Women attack female transgressors and men the males. You, and children like you, without an extended family, form a loose collective of revenge. To be powerful is essential for urban survival. The power structure is codified. If you wear designer clothes then you are deemed to be a capable fighter. The sub-text is, sadly, that everyone knows there is no money to buy the clothes by legitimate means, so they must have been acquired illegally. Stolen, robbed from someone, or paid for by illegally acquired money.

It took me some time to understand why you would not wear normal clothes. The trend had so established itself that a lot of the kids were wearing the price tags as part of the outfit, displaying their capacity for acquiring wealth, very much as the rich buy houses and posh cars. But these clothes afforded you children who were usually excluded from the centre of power momentary dignity. Wearing these clothes, you could be walking down the posh streets of London and not be out of place. You became one of the many consumers having the privilege of safety.

In this power structure the "hoodie" (tracksuit-top with hood) was an essential accessory for safety. Middle-class shoppers believed the hoodie wearer to be targeting them, but the truth is the hoodie is a hideout. Most of you expect an attack on the street. A retribution for the harm you may have caused, so you use the disguise to conceal yourselves from the assailant.

By fifteen or sixteen, many of you hide in the bonnet of your illegally acquired cars. No driving licence, dodgy insurance, M.O.T. and tax discs, but the car is safer. Its speed delivers you to outer London destinations. The drug-trade graduates. You begin by pedalling on bikes, and move on to rented or stolen vehicles. The business upgrades with your cars. There's less seeking of child victims for robbery. In fact most of you feed the younger children on your estates with donations of £1 for burgers. The memory of yourselves as starving and desperate children is not long faded.

The police watch you all grow up with a mixture of perverse fascination, understanding and admiration. They don't forget you have drug addicted mothers, having found you as toddlers playing with the drug measuring scales, crawling about looking for morsels of care. It is a tragedy which does not need to happen.

The politicians talk of respect. Where were they when you were a little boy without the bus fare? When they had tea in the commons, your belly rumbled with hunger. The society they preserve delivers the cycle of overpowering threats you were exposed to from a young age. They sustain their sense of social potency – they can talk, debate, and mobilize and moralize resources. You talked, begged, and then you realized the society where you live delivers through violence.

You want legitimacy as much as the men in suits do. You did not choose this desperation to be born into. Your home and street environment conspired to violence, to the distribution of hate as justice. They should respect you for the shreds of tenderness you managed to preserve amidst the devastation. Their laws to you are pathetic. The lawyers peddle just as much truthlessness except it is disguised in intellectual legitimacy. You boys sit in court watching how the law can be manipulated to give you all a legal release. The truth is compromised either way. You lie to survive, the state lies to show mental agility in negotiating the volumes of legal argument. How can you trust this society? Your conspiracy theories feel well justified to you.

The most frightening aspect of your story may be that you are not abnormal. Your capacity for murder, a product of your murdered childhood. Maybe your psychology is appropriate to your environment. Maybe you are well adapted to survive. For you to emerge unable to kill or fight might have been more psychologically alarming. I do not think you are a sociopath, inappropriate in your social and emotional exchanges; on the contrary, you are well adapted to the violence which surrounds you, which is perpetrated against and by you to ensure survival.

You once told me that on the street if you are seen as powerless you will always be prey to someone more powerful. The street communication is viral. If you let some injustice pass by unchecked, your reputation is at risk, your status diminished. No one will defend you, your friends and acquaintances are equally preoccupied with their own survival. You are the sole guardian of your own safety. You are your own security camera, your own police, your own judge. You have to be because you live in a ghetto where legitimate power failed you all. The law creators hide behind their security gates. The money makers move in bullet-proof cars. Their laws are good for them. Where you live in the underbelly of desperation, another law prevails. Its fundamental tenet is not to be seen to lose power, or you lose your life.

It is paradoxical this struggle to survive. It is reduced itself, to the basest level of humanity. To ensure physical survival a psychological death has to take place. You have to die within before you can become violent enough to survive without.

You have a spiritual dimension despite all this. Something of a quality remains. I cannot call it love, I do not know if there is any left, but I think it may be compassion. Perhaps you have more compassion than the politician who so easily dismisses you as a social reject. Maybe you have a depth of understanding more profound than the academic philosopher. Maybe you have more emotional intelligence than the psychiatrist who seeks you for his secure wards. Maybe you have something we all need to learn. Maybe I am right not to be afraid provided I do not violate your efforts to self-preserve. But I want something better for you than mere survival. Your intelligence is beautiful. I want to give you a most important gift denied you. I want you to have the ability to dream your future.

When I read this letter to you, your response initially was: "It's all right, really". Over and over again you kept laughing in recognition. I felt like crying. There was such intensity in your attention when you listened. Later you sent me a text saying: "I love you. From Mr Mason".

To find out more about the issues covered in this letter, please refer to Chapter 7, Cradled in Terror: Children's Capacity to be Violent, p.91.

CHAPTER 6

Psychosocial Vulnerabilities Leading to Violence

Letter to Rocky

DEAR ROCKY,

Today you rang from prison using your secret mobile phone. Sitting out a nine-year sentence can get very lonely. No one is visiting you in some jail somewhere far away. But you like prison. It is safe, it is better than home has ever been for you. I told you about writing this letter, an apology to children who had been hurt. You were surprised that anyone would say sorry about your sad childhood.

This letter had to be written to Rocky – the fighter, the deliverer of a mean punch. On the phone you talked of your poetry. You are writing a book about love. You loved your mother and she loved you. From the prison you express gratitude for all she has done, but you were beyond her control.

There was always something electric about you. Even your hair stood up wild, alert, like you it was frenzied and unbound. Sometimes you would stick a comb into it like a cool fashion accessory. You were dangerous, a tantrum could result in someone's death. You were like a volcano smoking, and a final explosion would release a lava of terror, red-hot fury engulfing everything in its path. The other children kept saying you were mad, but you were no madder than the rest. You were prepared to kill and considered prison a resting place.

Your father was a drug addict who developed schizophrenia and eventually committed suicide. Every so often in your darkest moments you would sigh with despair, wondering if madness was also your destiny. Your mother, a kind woman, moved in with your step-father. Very early on he began battering her. Your earliest memory is of being about four years old. He hurled you to the wall and broke your skull for blood. You ended up in hospital. Who knows what this injury did to your little brain, but emotionally the man scarred you for life. After this event, you remember destroying all your toys, smashing them like your skull had been smashed.

Schools could not cope with your restlessness. Your mother felt ashamed of your behaviour. Everyone who came into contact with you burdened her with complaints. She did not want you either, out of sheer exhaustion, but the love was always there. Three more children were born into this household, two of them twins, and all of them girls. On the phone from prison you tell me they are giving your mother a hard time, going out all night, but she is too proud to ask for help. I remember your fury devastating her house. You broke every door, every piece of furniture. Nothing was spared your rage. Your elderly grandfather tried to help but you were beyond his comprehension. Social services paraded in and out with their files. The special educational and behavioural disturbance facility of the local authority could not cope. No one knew what led to your unfathomable rages.

I could prevent the eruption by holding your hand, talking to you as you stuttered with Tourettes. Obscenities escaped the hatch and I continued holding your hand until the storm abated. Sometimes I stood in front of your weapons, knowing in a moment I could get stabbed. In seeing me protect the other children from your rage, you began to trust me. You would seek me out, sit next to me, draw pictures and attempt to write. You could barely form any letters at fifteen. At sixteen you turned to drug dealing, having started using cannabis at the special boarding school. The drugs made you more crazed. You drove around on motorbikes, touchingly harbouring pictures of all those you loved in the seat enclosure.

The day and night mixed. Your chaotic life became more volatile, more sinister. You stole cars, you stole properties, you robbed, nowhere was a resting place. You seemed to be losing your mind. Often you would hallucinate a little orange cat and then tell me about it. Sometimes you would talk to the cat and ask that I would participate. The cat, you thought, told you your salvation was in making money, rising above poverty. The cat became your soul mate and your nemesis.

Your criminal activity escalated but the youth courts kept sending you to youth offending programmes and they could not cope. You smashed tables. The police would be sent for because you were holding the teams hostage. When I was in the room you were somewhat verbally abusive, but you were calm, and you sat next to me, leaning your head on my shoulder, a child once more. Your attachment to me was significant and you sought it out in order to help yourself acquire some peace. I felt overwhelmed as all the agencies shut their doors in your face. The housing department would not house you as you were a risk to other residents and landlords. The youth offending teams avoided their responsibility to care for you. No college would take you, and your days yawned from one to the next. You played with your drug rounds, your multiple phone lines, making money and then smoking it. You were hungry, unkempt. Sometimes you slept in enclosures of dustbins. Sometimes you told of how a frustrated police officer and his mates had taken you to the basement of some building and battered you for an injustice done to them. Every day some atrocity was perpetrated by you and against you. We tried to help you every day, placing you in one hotel after another. Sometimes you would manage yourself for one night, at other times the hotels would call us to remove you. Most of the local hotels and bed and breakfasts were refusing to take you. We were running out of accommodation. We were glad that a hotel with a large number of asylum seekers had been prepared to offer you a room, but that lasted no more than three days. You had threatened the hotel worker with a gun and stolen the money in the hotel's till.

Every day the forensic psychiatrist and I spoke on the phone. He was a special man, kind but frightened. He was frightened of the structures around him. Frightened that he would get penalized if he failed with one of his disturbed patients, and you were disturbed; but somewhere deep down, like me, he understood your childlikeness. Often he would comment how you had managed to find some calm with me, some way of being regulated through our attachment relationship.

You presented with a lot of paradoxes. Sometimes you would feel suicidal and out of control. The local hospital's emergency department would be on alert, the psychiatric unit thought you were dangerous. We would arrive together and the entire contents of your pockets had to be emptied. They were seeking weapons and invariably you had them. Sometimes you would hide them in the bushes.

I remember leaving you on a plastic sofa at one of these units. You were so exhausted and so dangerous that they had decided to section you. Your section was in the highest secure unit, but within twelve hours you had smashed the fire exit door and escaped back into the community. The hospital rang me in a frenzy, hoping you would turn up and like a little boy you did. Often I would bribe you with Chinese takeaways so that we could go back to the hospital.

Once we sat in a car with you carrying a massive baseball bat. Our destination – the appointment with your forensic psychiatrist. You insisted I come to every meeting with you and sit calmly in a chair to assist the clinician to reach you somewhere beyond the chaos you perpetrated.

The forensic psychiatrist, a small man, sat in his leather chair, ready for you and me to sit down. You approached him with your baseball bat, stood behind the chair, and told him that if he did not get up to offer me the chair then you would hit him. He promptly obliged!

You were so full of surprises, on the one hand concerned, on the other lethally dangerous. But it was not always just the harm you caused to others. You were subjected to great harm too. Once I heard that you had been kidnapped. I was frantic to find you. You emerged twenty-four hours later. They had burnt your skin using a car lighter and cigarette lighters. You had been battered with baseball bats, your ribs damaged, your skull yet again split open. I was horrified by the attack. You were paranoid and terrified that your assailants would seek you out again. I could not understand what injustice had been perpetrated against you and what you had done to deserve it, but the street's rules require a redress for a wrong and your wrong was to have stolen their drug business.

You were couriering for the men and on this occasion you decided to keep the goods and the money. They wanted them back, and for this they burnt your skin. Sometimes the damage was unbearable. I was so tired, so worried about balancing out the care you needed with the danger you posed. I constantly talked to the police on the phone, discussing the level of risk, and they in turn talked to me whenever they were looking for you, after the latest crime you had committed. But we had an agreement, the police and me. They would not arrest you on our premises. They knew that Kids Company was your sanctuary and they wanted to keep you safe.

One of your crimes eventually resulted in your being hospitalized in a psychiatric hospital. This was the first time someone had begun to look at your mental health issues, without constantly thinking of you as a risk to the general public. The hospital was a place of safety, and the Chinese psychiatrist and I used to talk, your mental condition a puzzle to us. He could not decide whether you were schizophrenic or sociopathic. He could not decide what your little orange cat was about. He could not comprehend your hyper-agitation alongside your tremendous empathy. Eventually you were released, the diagnosis uncertain.

When they released you, and each time they let you out of prison, they left you with no money, and no accommodation organized. You walked back onto the streets, having to survive. Each time, very rapidly, you ended up resorting to your drug dealing and your drug taking. The final deliverance to prison was when the police were chasing you down and you shot at them. This time they caught you, and for this you are sitting in prison doing your nine-year prison sentence.

It makes me wonder how many such vulnerable individuals end up in the penal system, the alternative psychiatric setting where the most excluded, the most vulnerable, and the most marginalized are offered sanctuary under the umbrella of a punishment. In prison there is no therapy. In prison the deep questions about why you caused such harm are not really asked, but prison gives you food, prison gives you a bed. Prison gives you an experience of discipline, a substitute paternal experience so lacking in your life and in the life of many other similarly disturbed children. Each time you have been in prison you have rung us weekly. Kids Company, your alternative family, the only agency which has had the stamina to stand by you despite the havoc you cause.

You are not the only desperate child turning to violence and dampening down your passion through drugs. There are thousands of you in local authorities in urban and depleted areas, but for you little boys there is no help. Every door closes as resources are too limited to assist you.

The kind psychiatrist kept up his end of the bargain. When you could not make it to hospital, he would meet us at the coffee shop and drink China tea. The sight of you, me and him with this delicacy was comical. You loved these tender moments, you loved being cared for.

You explained to me that what drove you crazy, what made you more and more dangerous, was that you had gone to the sexual health clinic. You had caught so many sexual transmitted diseases that they told you that you would never be able to have children. From prison, you described how this thought drove you to the brink of madness, but now you have two children, with two different baby mothers, and I ask you how you are coping. Humorously you tell me, "By not seeing either of them".

It is so hard to tell what the future will bring for you. You remain untreated for the devastating traumas of your life. Because you have been labelled a sociopath, the prison system is going to be your ultimate destination, as no psychiatric provision will now treat you. Your love poems suggest there is feeling there. Your love of your mother suggests there is attachment there. The sociopath label is too easy.

Today scraps of paper arrived from the prison. They are your autobiography. Pages of sadness, the honesty of which was too unbearable. I am sorry.

The Sunset *by Rocky*

The sun setting on a hot summer's day only can take my breath away, 'cos I can only see as far as the bars on my cage.

I wish I didn't have to live like a slave. Just to see the sunset through a small hole; it's like my eyes seeing gold!

But once the sun has set and day has turned to night, the coldness that runs through my body don't give me a reason to fight to turn my luck around, not see the sunset run me into the ground.

To find out more about the issues covered in this letter, please refer to Chapter 7, Cradled in Terror: Children's Capacity to be Violent, p.91.

Cradled in Terror: Children's Capacity to be Violent

INFANTS INCUBATED IN violence grow up to become children and young people who are capable of extreme harm. The genesis of violence is sinister in its creeping development. It begins often with a vulnerable infant seeking attachment and attunement from its mother. A sensitive caregiver reflects back the existence of the infant through the capacity to be in tune with the child's needs. The mother soothes, stimulates, feeds and nurtures her child. The dance of need and response forms a breathtaking duet, fine-tuned to levels of sensitivity which are almost magical. Through the loving gaze of its mother, a cared-for infant has his or her existence affirmed.

The positive effects of loving care have been instinctively understood throughout history, but now the machinery of science is shedding more confirmatory light on its importance. Science has a range of devices available to it in order to be able to acquire a better understanding of brain functioning. The MRI (Magnetic Resonance Imaging) scan is capable of showing the structures of the brain, and a functional MRI scan (fMRI) is capable of showing the brain's activities. Through the PET (Positron Emission Tomography) scan, we can show the chemical activities of the brain using dyes. We are capable of picking up the brain's electrical activity by using EEGs (Electroencephalograms). The combination of sophisticated brain scanning machines and hormone measurements has resulted in our beginning to understand better the chemistry of terror. Early research is demonstrating that the capacity to control behaviour and make pro-social choices is very much dependent on the efficient and balanced functioning of the brain. Minute damage or neurochemical depletion may play a significant role in violence.

The general public is often shocked by children's violence. The normal response has understandably been one of seeking justice, accountability and retribution in the form of punishment. The basic assumption is that the violent individual makes a morally poor choice, either in allowing their temper to be lost, or in acting out violent behaviour, which is seen as anti-social. However, the problem may be more complex.

Violence has its origins in both personal factors and social factors. Social factors determine the apparatus and methodology of violence. If the prevalent weapon in a neighbourhood is a knife, then stab wounds are higher. If it is a gun, then more people are shot. Sometimes violence is used as a secondary tool to robberies or acquisition of goods. It is exercised therefore with premeditation and control, provided things do not get out of hand. An example of this is the security van of a bank being held up, with the threat of killing.

Some individuals expressing violence are labelled sociopaths, previously known as psychopaths. Their violence typically does not stem from a loss of temper; it is usually premeditated and intricately planned, yet void of emotions. In fact, sociopaths are thought not to experience empathy, nor to have access to genuine emotions.

Some clinicians believe this is a defence mechanism evolving as a result of infantile trauma. Others believe this inability to feel stems from a personality disorder, which is created as a result of poor parental care. There are those who consider the sociopathic condition a byproduct of brain developmental issues, as in developmental disorders like autism.

What the public has not really been aware of is that violence may emanate from trauma. Violence which is trauma-triggered has the characteristic of being impulsive and not so premeditated. All human beings have bad experiences. Those who are traumatized describe bad experiences as being catastrophically overpowering, for example being involved in an accident or witnessing a friend being shot dead and not being able to intervene. An experience of trauma does not have to have involved one event only. It can be an accumulation of numerous events which are cumulatively referred to as complex trauma.

Trauma is a stress response gone wrong. Most of us experience terror, overcome or escape it, then calm down from it and then the intensity of memory and feeling around the event diminishes. The traumatized individual gets stuck in the response and in the process.

The individual who is stuck in a traumatic cycle is described as suffering from post-traumatic stress disorder (PTSD). A PTSD-sufferer often experiences flashbacks, which are frozen memories of the traumatic event.

Post-traumatic stress disorder

Some individuals suffering from PTSD have a store of visual and/or sensory images and feelings. They may repeatedly recall smells or visual images related to the trauma as flashbacks. These frequently play themselves back in their mind's eye, but without leading to any resolution. Sometimes memories and flashbacks lead to hair-trigger impulsive and violent reactions.

There is substantial debate about whether the propensity to violence is genetic. The professionals have differing views, but it is difficult to settle the argument, because the propensity for violence could be established while the baby is in the womb, by virtue of the stress chemicals the baby is exposed to, as a result of the mother being distressed and worried. The chronic exposure to maternal distress, combined with the mother's poor care capacities, may disturb the brain function and chemistry of the infant, making her more vulnerable to stress reactions and violent expressions. Some believe that the altered behaviour of genes also has an impact.

Chemical vulnerabilities to violence are referred to as stemming from personal factors, though they still require environmental factors such as upbringing to be expressed. It is possible for a child to be born neurochemically sensitive to stress and violence, but if their care condition is good and subsequent attachments robust, then this infant is likely to overcome, or not express violently, their personal propensity to rageful reactions. The outcome is poor for children who have been exposed to chemical stresses in the womb, who have poor attachment relationships, minimal resilience and then live in conditions where they are exposed to violent acts. Violence is more prevalent in the family home.

More children witness domestic violence and are harmed and sexually abused by families than by strangers. External conditions such as poverty, housing and environmental stresses do, however, also play a part in diminishing both maternal and infant resilience to violence.

The development of the capacity for violence

The human infant is born with substantial neuronal capacity, although it is thought some of it is dormant. A child's first experiences of communication with the maternal care giver are what brings to life the emotional development of her brain. The brains of mothers and babies have been simultaneously scanned and an extraordinary synchronicity of activity has been identified in the two brains. Love and care also release endorphins, which are pleasure-giving brain chemicals. When the infant is cared for and reflected back appropriately, both mother and baby display enhanced brain activity, which leads to mutual pleasure.

Sometimes the mother fails in her sensitivity. A well cared-for baby can tolerate this failure in attunement and recover from it. For the child who has acquired the capacity to delay gratification without feeling persecuted, a repertoire of hope is facilitated. The child tolerates moments of frustration believing the mother will return to her soothing function.

Many children are, sadly, exposed to chronic failures in care giving. At a milder end, this is represented by a preoccupied, depressed or substance addicted mother whose capacity to hold her baby's needs in mind is impaired. The mother is too absorbed in her own survival or impoverishment. She has no emotional resources to meet the child's needs appropriately. The baby feels catastrophically dropped out of the mother's caring mind. The mother's mindfulness, which should have held mother and infant in a diad, is no longer holding the baby safe. The infant experiences distress which is not relieved. Some babies protest and cry, others feel even protest is too hopeless and they sink into an apathetic silence, a deadly unresponsiveness. Both the distressed child and the apathetic baby display high levels of the stress hormone cortisol which is thought to act like an acid in the brain and is believed to kill off some of the brain's important neuronal pathways, including those responsible for pro-social responses and working memory.

On the one hand, there is the destruction of some key neuronal structures. On the other, those neuronal pathways which are waiting to be activated, brought to life, and to form connections with other pathways, fail to do so. Lack of appropriate communication, lack of attunement and lack of stimulation mean that neuronal pathways are not able to come alive through use. In neurobiological and physiological terms, the unnurtured child lacks resilience. Her communication repertoire is more limited, as it has not been used to a maximum level. She has less resilience against stress. Sometimes there are disturbances in her cortisol levels, including both under- and overproduction, or they have too many cortisol receptors and thus an over-efficient response to stress. The infant's hope repertoire is impoverished because her experience is that the maternal care giver never returned to the position of good care giving. She remained remote and distant. Brain science is currently exploring the impact of chronic stress on the functioning of the prefrontal lobe from which control capacities are thought to emanate.

Children as witnesses of extreme violence

The challenges of being emotionally abandoned represent one dimension of the problem. The other presents itself in children who have been exposed to extremes of violence. As a young infant, these offspring are observers of family horror. They sit and watch while horrific violence unfolds around them. They describe years later how they witnessed their mothers kicked, dragged across the floor or bottles smashed over their fathers' skulls. Sometimes these children crawl through the debris of drugs, desperate at the non-availability of escape. As young boys and girls they may at times attempt to intervene to prevent the catastrophe. But they realize how powerless they are as their efforts do not diminish the blows. These children store the memory of every act of violence. Some have these scenes played back to them, as their mind reproduces the images, smells, sensations and sounds in flashbacks.

Flashbacks are unprocessed, because they were too overpowering at the time to be diluted in their impact through the process of thinking. These flashbacks to horrific experiences are beyond the capacity of the individual to mentalize, that is, mentally metabolize them. They are a history of violence, which returns time and time again, demanding a resolution.

Traumatized children can repeatedly be re-traumatized through their own flashbacks, night terrors and their own violent actions. The mental wall between "now" and "then" is too thin and horror seeps through every fabric of mental defence to interfere with their day-to-day thinking.

Children exposed to extremes of violence and abuse, especially when it is physical and sexual, store the events not only on a psychological level, but also on a physiological level. The trauma remains in the cells of the body like an encoded shock waiting to be unleashed. On a physiological level the terrorized child is relentlessly secreting adrenalin, which triggers the release of a similar flight–fright hormone called noradrenalin. Had there been a robust attachment relationship in place, maybe the child could have been able to call upon the experiences of good care given by a maternal carer to calm down or self-soothe. But poorly attached infants do not bring resilience into their childhood and are therefore doubly disadvantaged by violence and neglect.

From victim to perpetrator of violence

Initially, the child is a victim, passively soaking up the violence. The images imprint themselves on the brain and on the body memory capacities. The child is further humiliated by not being able to effect any change through their protest or begging. As well as being survivors of violence, children often report observing themselves during it. The most violently abused children describe how they experienced themselves "hovering above themselves", as they watched the abuser abuse them. The sensation of detaching from the body is a form of depersonalization, a defence of detachment. The child may "split off" an aspect of themselves in order to protect a portion of the personality, as if to preserve some aspect of the self from being perverted through the process of abuse. It could also be a form of pain management or a protection against being overwhelmed.

Some children feel so disconnected that they sometimes complain of not being able to "feel themselves as existing". Sometimes these children may resort to self-harm in order to effect a return to reality. It is as if physical pain rekindles a sense of existing in them. Sometimes self-harm shifts the pain from an emotional and invisible space to a physical and visible space. The child may watch the blood flowing and experience calm from observing its movement on the skin.

Children who have been partly detached while being abused become very sensitive to humiliation. They not only remember being violated, but they also act as an audience witnessing their own pleading for the violence to stop. A memory of themselves is stored as a begging and "pathetic victim", as well as a humiliated being. The "split-off" aspect of them saw it – so did the abuser. The child hates having shared the perception of themselves as a victim with the abuser.

This hatred towards the victim can find expression years later, when the young child has grown to be an adolescent; potentially she is physically strong enough to have made the transition from a "pathetic victim" to a "powerful perpetrator". Some children seek revenge. They harm their abusers and those who facilitated the abuse, if their care is not dependent on them. Some turn the hate inwards and harm themselves violently. A sense of repulsion and disgust conspires to destroy the vulnerable child within them. Tenderness and sensitivity are perceived as weaknesses. These children often make an unconscious resolution never to be vulnerable again. That is, if their spirit is not entirely crushed and some capacity to survive remains within them.

The severely abused child may fragment their personality into split-off aspects at times. They may play the whore, the bully, the gangster and the abuser as almost caricature personalities. The splitting reduces conflict and gives the illusion that they have greater mastery over their identity and expression. Sometimes the invasion by the perpetrator is so abusive that any sense of self is eradicated.

For some children the memory of abuse and family violence combines with an incapacity to self-regulate and regulate the emotions. These young people often have a build-up of energy which seeks release, they are hyper-aroused. They may actively look for a victim and find release through an act of violence. Often these perpetrators of violence cannot tolerate pleading in their victims, because the begging repulses them and reminds them of the humiliation they experienced as young children being subjected to abuse. They despise victims who ask for mercy and want to obliterate them, in order to suffocate and silence the powerless child within them. In children who self-harm by cutting themselves, the victim may represent an aspect of themselves.

Children and young people who have been repeatedly violated and abused may shift from a state of terror to one of exhaustion. Sometimes adrenal tests show the physiological explanation for this energylessness lies in adrenal exhaustion and the unavailability of cortisol. It is as if the hyper-aroused thermostat has made a shift to an under-aroused state. The primitive brain is on alert and reacts quickly and forcefully to ensure survival, sometimes at all costs. Often the most innocent exchanges or facial expressions can be misinterpreted as potential attacks or humiliation, triggering the traumatized individual into feelings of rage.

Usually non-violent individuals are left wondering how a young person could react so aggressively and cause such mindless violence. The answer is that the harm is not done in a state of mindfulness or thinking. It is a desperate and pre-programmed biological response which is activated through physiological arousal responses and body memories. These body memories generate energy, seeking resolution and release.

Types of violence

As we have seen, there are two forms of violence expressed by the traumatized child. One is planned and premeditated. Its origin is hate and revenge or the acquisition of goods. The victim is identified coldly, pursued and systematically harmed. The harm can be physical, psychological or sometimes sexual. Sometimes the capacity for violence arouses sexual feelings and is eroticized. This type of perpetrator is sexually aroused and satisfied through sexually violent acts. They may repeat the trauma by adopting a masochistic position or they may act sadistically. Often roles can also be interchanged.

The premeditated violator is organized in his abuse. He plans, implements and covers his tracks. The violence has a compulsive and repetitive feel to it, as the trauma is repeatedly re-enacted in new disguises. The root of its genesis is an uncontainable build-up of negative energy seeking release, the byproduct of emotional pain, which has been perverted.

Violent behaviours emerge when there has been no soothing or kindness. The victim has not been afforded a return to the centre of society through loving care. The perverted individual lives in the shadows of love, secretly seeking to be embraced, but believing himself to be too repulsive and foul to be chosen. If he can have no access to legitimate love then he might as well steal emotional space illegitimately.

The second form of violence expressed by traumatized individuals is not so premeditated, but can be triggered, sometimes unwittingly. Its power is catastrophic and the perpetrator is often shocked by his own behaviour, when they are calm enough to ponder its impact. It takes approximately ninety minutes from trigger to calm-down-point for this type of violence (this is provided there are no other triggers in between).

With the unmeditated violence, "threat" is the trigger. The threat can be either a physical risk or a risk of suffering indignity. A humiliating situation where the individual is experiencing a loss of power is enough to trigger stored memories of being catastrophically powerless as a child, and its consequent public shame. Once the trigger has evoked the response, there is an automatic response which gets acted out no matter what the appropriateness or gravity of the situation.

This is the young man who feels "dissed" (disrespected) and ends up murdering the offender, or the young boy stuck in a traffic jam being shouted at, who smashes a brick over a woman's head. The experience is one of the perpetrator having been "tipped over" into a physiologically hyper-aroused state with no internal capacities to modify their own response.

This type of violence feels automatic. The individual is often detached, acting like a robot in his fury. The perpetrator of this type of violence is often seen to be breathless, sweating, their pupils dilated and sometimes shaking – all of these symptoms suggest an adrenal hyper-arousal. Cortisol levels are elevated and usually take a long time to go back to a normal baseline.

Impaired capacity for empathy

Children who have been exposed to high levels of violence without being afforded comfort or compassion are often empathically incapacitated. In not being able to feel for themselves, they forget what it feels like to feel. They walk in an emotionally numb world, believing others within it to be equally void of tenderness. Their only access to feelings is violence or terror, both in inflicting it and in being defended against it. Emotionally cold children are sustained in their frozenness because those around them do not perceive them to be inviting an emotional response. Few people dare pinch the cheeks of the "cold child" and tell him how cute he is. The emotionally numb child is unwittingly confirmed in his or her worldview, because those around him do not react with tenderness towards him. Often, they avoid contact with this type of child. Fear becomes the tool for alienation. The child alienates potential carers by exhibiting great violence and carers seek distance as they are horrified by the breach in boundaries of safety.

Violated children cannot tolerate boundaries. They either perceive them as rejection, hence humiliation, or discard them as without meaning. These children often have disturbances in body boundaries. Either they are excessively distant-seeking or rigid, or they invade people's personal space, very much as their own space was violated.

The inability to access tenderness and feeling makes the child unable to experience compassion for himself. He does not feel sorrow for the child within himself who has been harmed. Neither can he feel sorrow for a victim he has hurt. The incapacity to access feelings for self and others disables his ability to anticipate the victim's feelings. In fact, we know through brain scanning mechanisms that the ability to anticipate the other person's feelings emanates from the same area of the brain as the ability to perceive yourself in the future and to hold a goal in mind. All anticipatory pro-social capacities are diminished. In not being able to feel sorrow for themselves and the victim, these children cannot experience empathy.

Often they are aware of not feeling anything. They may even worry about being so emotionally numb. However, they are vigilant enough to recognize how much empathy is a requirement of social interaction. Sometimes restorative justice sessions, where victim and perpetrator come face-to-face with each other, may rekindle some capacity to feel in the child, who sees the victim's upset directly. But all too often these young people go through the motions of apologizing without genuine remorse. To feel remorse, empathy has to be accessed first. In not being able to experience tenderness for himself, the perpetrator cannot access empathy or engage in genuine remorse.

The management of violent behaviour

For this type of child, punishment is not an efficient learning tool. The terrorized child has had experiences of extreme violation and horror. There is nothing more one can do to them which would frighten them into behaving better. Punishment is a redundant solution, because its impact is no greater than that of the horrors which have already taken place. Many of these youngsters also have impaired memory capacities. They expel noxious stimuli and they cannot store a mild negative stimulus such as would be felt in the internalized threat of punishment to call upon it in order to prevent themselves from misbehaving the next time they are about to commit an offence. Those who learn to adapt in response to the process of punishment usually have an organized psyche, which can sustain a cause and effect link.

The violated child is emotionally too disorganized to make the necessary connections and learn from the infliction of punishment. The violated child lives in a different emotional universe from the rest of us. Their sense of personal damage is so profound that mild threats of damage like punishment do not register with them. The only thing which controls their behaviour momentarily (by making them afraid and frozen) is the possibility of violence which threatens their survival. I have often watched as an excessively aggressive child is frozen in watchfulness as someone more violent than them is hovering about.

Social implications of violence

Society often asks if punishment would modify these violent children's behaviours. How can we control the damage these children cause? And what is the long-term impact on society? The management of violence has to be the most urgent task on our national agenda. We talk of terrorism and the threats of violence perpetrated by extremists and fundamentalists. Yet it is my view that the greatest terrorism lurks behind closed doors. It is the terrorization of children who then grow to terrorize in revenge.

This cycle of abuse is not simply expressed through human interaction. Recent studies in genetics suggest that experiences of violence can have a long-term impact on which aspects of the genome are expressed.

A hyper-aroused, disturbed teenager goes on to give birth to a deregulated infant, who is both impacted by the mother's psychological trauma, but also by her physiological trauma residues and the conditions of intrauterine stress expression.

So if violence is not addressed and prevented within one generation, its impact will be felt across the next generation too and trauma, like a legacy, is inherited to sustain the damage.

Social tolerance of violence has to be addressed robustly. The American "broken window syndrome" is an apposite analogy. The thinking behind it is that society should have zero tolerance of violence and be seen to robustly address it when it takes place. This type of intervention starves the perpetrator of violence. The violence is an emotional state seeking environmental expression. If environmental factors are removed, then the opportunity for violence in public places is minimized, as are any external triggers which may perpetuate physiological violence capacities. Addressing environmental violence ensures that psychological violence is not facilitated as an adaptive response.

Environmental measures on their own do not prevent violence. They simply drive it behind closed doors or underground. To reduce violence within society, the approach has to be environmental, social, cultural, interpersonal and personal with the emphasis being on interpersonal and personal. It must begin with the teaching of parents-to-be about the necessity for attunement with their infants. Parents must be helped to take on board the complex psychological responsibility of parenting.

Since excellence in parenting is essentially an emotional task, it is entirely dependent on the individual parent's well-being, both physical and psychological. A depressed or hyper-agitated mother will fail in being sensitive to her infant's needs. It therefore becomes imperative to help children and young people who present with psychosocial distresses before they become parents.

Yet personal psychological states can never be separated from environmental and social factors. Poverty, poor housing, poor special educational needs interventions, inaccessibility of therapeutic services all increase psychological vulnerability and lead to its becoming entrenched. Children's violence cannot be relegated to the peripheries of newspaper horror reporting. It has to be a central agenda for which we all take responsibility. Violence is the byproduct of a society with social malaise and every citizen needs to accept responsibility for effecting a recovery.

For the traumatized child frozen emotionally by the absence of love and the experience of humiliation, there is a need to take revenge and there is a storage of hate. Punishment is experienced as rejection, which deepens the child's resentment. The only hope is to find love for this child. The only thing which can return them from the abyss is the capacity to rekindle their ability to feel, by feeling for them. We have to rise above their defences and gently care for them so that the wound of having been abandoned to the experience of violation can be healed. Once these children feel contained and consistent love they will not want to lose it.

Path to recovery

The path to recovery is a treacherous one. At first, this type of child will seek out your love. Then they will get terrified of it and fearful of losing it, believing you to be withdrawing it imminently. They bring about a rupture in the attachment before you can. Working with a violated child can feel like an assault on your feelings and psyche. Sometimes their sheer cruelty is breathtaking and shocking. Sometimes they seek to humiliate others just as they were humiliated. Sometimes the most benign events assume significance as they are symbolically used in the service of triggering traumatic memories.

The violent child seeks proximity and simultaneously rejects it as though this paradoxical behaviour has been programmed into the very fabric of their being. Sometimes, in order to manage flashbacks and emotional pain, children may resort to substance misuse as a form of self-medication. This usually plunges them into an extremely dangerous, violent world, as they attempt to acquire their drugs. Loving this type of child is challenging.

Interventions addressing violence

Practical interventions are needed in parallel with the task of loving. The hyper-aroused physiology and addiction to adrenalin requires careful management. The storage of physical trauma and accumulated unexpressed energy requires physical outlets. Sports which facilitate hard contact or managed risks are usually a good outlet. Boxing, squash, tennis, go-karting, dodgem cars which can be smashed into each other, running treadmills, strenuous activity in the gym all enable the children to express pent-up potentially violent energy. But these need to be followed up by a calming activity. Alternative health therapies like massage, acupuncture (if they can tolerate the needle), osteopathy, aromatherapy, facials, saunas and swimming are all good calming activities. Avoiding stimulants in food can assist the process.

Many of the expressive arts are also very useful, although they need to be exercised in a special way with the traumatized child. Often the capacity to imagine is impoverished in the child who has been exposed to extremes of terror. They can exercise fantasy around revenge or acts of violence, but beyond this they often draw a blank.

The request to produce a creative product can be experienced as persecutory and potentially trigger humiliation or flight responses. For the imagination to work, there must be enough stillness and tranquillity for mental play to take place. The traumatized child is often unable to play creatively and cannot produce creative artistic outcomes. The practitioner needs to provide the elementary tools for these children to develop or manipulate into their own personalized expressions. Just as toddlers need their hands held for the first steps to be activated, so the traumatized child requires creative handholding to be able to create. The depersonalization defence adopted by many of these children mirrors back at them an experience of themselves which feels to them like a sense of profound emptiness. The vacuousness in turn is experienced as shameful. So both in fine arts and performing arts, they require a starting point and assistance, so collage and colouring in pictures may be easier than an imaginative composition.

The advantage of drama is that children can practise different psychological states through different roles. This simultaneously affords them safety in distance, but also allows them to experiment with feelings which they may wish to take on board on the way to a widening emotional repertoire, beyond violence and humiliation. It is as if through physical action and role-play the areas of the brain which have remained dormant or have not been allowed to develop can, through the process of repetition, be allowed to develop or be brought to life for the first time. The physical arts are also especially useful, as they allow for expression of physiologically stored energy and trauma memory residues.

Pharmacological interventions

Very little research has been done into potential pharmacological interventions. There is now a recognition that many children diagnosed with Attention Deficit Hyperactivity Disorder may in fact be suffering from PTSD and have been wrongly diagnosed. There is also a potential crossover between conduct disorders and post-traumatic disorders, as well as borderline disorders, with children either meeting the criteria of both diagnoses, or exhibiting poor behaviour control secondary to thermostatic impairment, as if trauma and the shock of it blew their system into disarray.

Children whose adrenals are exhausted, may exhibit affect withdrawal and shutdown. They may be diagnosed with depression. Depression and its treatment is often very complex in the traumatized child because she simultaneously needs mood elevation, but excessive agitation may mean she also requires energy controlling medication. A mixture of antidepressants, tranquilizing drugs and beta blockers is currently being used.

Trauma in children is a relatively new field, but one which is demanding urgent attention. The Romanian orphans, boy soldiers, children of wars, AIDS orphans, children of genocides and children who have had to survive on the streets are a growing population. In England and the United States alone, vast numbers of children live below poverty line. There are unacceptable levels of failure in youth offending programmes and custodial sentencing. At the same time there is a concomitant escalation in child abuse and neglect. Child violence is perceived as an epidemic with a potentially catastrophic impact on society. There are too many children on youth offending registers, and not enough on the child protection register. Many children on the youth offending register in the UK need re-classification. They need to be recognized as vulnerable children in need of protection who are seriously challenged by their own inability to regulate their physiological and emotional reactions. This is more a mental health issue than a moral flaw. There is even a risk that there will not be enough non-violent citizens to police morality. The only balm for this wound is to prevent the abuse of children and to offer tenderness and love within a robust structure so that they do not pass on the trauma to their offspring.

Violent children and therapeutic staff

For trauma recovery to be a national agenda, the workforce needs to be therapeutically trained. There is a need to return to care giving as a vocational and spiritually creative task. Mechanistic rituals of care which are heartless do not rekindle the capacity to feel, either in the care recipient or the caregiver. For appropriate feelings to be restored to the patient, the practitioner needs to model them and expose the child to them within safe limits she can tolerate.

The central therapeutic task is one of de-shaming and re-parenting. The child needs the blanket of shame removed. This is especially challenging when her bad behaviour needs boundarying or correction. Attempts at discipline are often experienced in a persecutory way by the traumatized child. They may recall to her the power imbalance of the adult perpetrator who had control over her. Challenges to negative behaviour can be delivered provided they are superseded by a recognition of the child as fundamentally good. A child who has hurt another in the playground may need to be told the following:

> "I really like you." (I am not rejecting you.)

> "I have noticed how kind you can be." (You can do good things.)

> "So I wondered what caused you to hurt that child." (Blame is placed within the cause rather than the child's self.)

> "I know you usually do not want to hurt people." (Increasing self-worth, so that there might be room to risk facing the negative behaviour.)

Usually an exchange like this de-shames the child sufficiently to allow for a respectful addressing of the negative behaviour. The child could then be helped to make reparation. Punishment is destructive and shames the child, potentially entrenching her further in the capacity to hate herself and others.

While therapeutic tasks need to be approached sensitively, there is a need for a robust structure which can be implemented when the child is in a state of hyper-arousal and is therefore potentially violent. The hyper-agitated child who has been traumatically triggered will often actively fail to hear what people say to her and may require restraint. If restraint is not sensitively carried out, it risks further engulfing the child into a state of hate and humiliation, as she feels overpowered yet again. So the restraint needs to be talked about as it is happening:

"We are not going to hurt you. We will just hold you gently, so that you don't hurt anyone and then regret it afterwards." (The child is described as good, because they are deemed as not wanting to hurt anyone, as demonstrated through a statement of their potential for regret.)

"We know you cannot control yourself right now, but please help us help you to achieve calm." (The child is empowered and engaged as a partner in the process, rather than being acted upon.)

As she begins to regain composure, the child needs to be praised and encouraged. She may feel very humiliated at being overpowered, so perhaps a little joke about how strong she is may restore some dignity and diminish her experience of herself as a victim. Those who have restrained the child need to make the effort to engage in a caring action subsequent to the restraint, for example bringing the child a drink or making her comfortable in some other way. Acts of gentleness and kindness serve to diminish any potential for the clinician to be aligned with the abusers of the past.

During restraint children may experience flashbacks. Any calming, soothing exchanges, including encouraging regular breathing, will help reduce the impact of the flashback.

Looking after the workers

In order for workers to be able to help in trauma recovery, they need to be looked after themselves. Otherwise they risk burnout, and secondary trauma as a result of witnessing the children's violence and being exposed to it. Weekly therapeutic supervision is an essential support structure and safety net, allowing for personal accumulation of negative energy to be soothed and released. Workers may experience triggering of their own personal painful material, which may require processing.

Workers need to be genuinely emotionally available to the traumatized child in order for the task of re-parenting to rekindle and facilitate a return to health. Just as PTSD is about a cycle of abuse, recovery is about a cycle of care. The child is cared for by a worker who is in turn looked after appropriately by management. Any compromise in quality risks re-traumatizing both the child and the worker, humiliating them both with the failure to respond to their needs. The task is one of compassionate and robust emotional holding while the psychophysiological storm passes, restoring calm. It is about many storms, many interventions and working towards longer lasting periods of homeostasis and spiritual calm. Only when traumatized children have achieved calm can they stop believing that they will die imminently, and start to believe that they can afford to think about their future.

Conclusion

The ability to hope facilitates the fundamental will to live. Sadly, too many violated children wish for death, as living seems worthless to them. Children who do not care if they live or die neither value themselves nor others. In their disregard they are thus immensely powerful and they may force their calmer peers to escalate their own behaviour in order to survive the potential havoc the violent child can cause.

Trauma intervention is a new field. In the past, the diagnosis of PTSD was given when the external event was deemed to be shocking, as in a car accident or rape. As the field advances we have acquired a more sophisticated understanding of trauma. It is now acknowledged that trauma can be accumulative and dependent on resilience factors within the individual. So, one traumatic event may not cause PTSD for an individual who has been well cared for and has resilience through attachment. The same event can completely fragment, overwhelm and lead to PTSD in an individual who has not been afforded resilience as a result of good childhood care.

The interplay between trauma and poor attachment relationships has been recognized as having an impact on resilience and recovery.

Love is the only experience which can make traumatized children hopeful again. It takes a whole community to nurture and protect a child and our sense of society can only emerge from honouring this responsibility collectively. It is no longer justifiable to blame traumatized children for what in effect is adults' failure to deliver good quality care. Science is already beginning to prove this point.

CHAPTER 8

Legitimate Neglect? Achieving the Best for Clients and Workers

Letter to Flower

DEAR FLOWER,

I am sorry you are not here to read this letter but justice demands that I write it.

I first met you in my office, your hip tilted as you struggled to walk. Despite being big you loved dancing and just before you died we made you a big ra-ra skirt. You loved it. You gave the performance of your life, dancing in front of 700 other students. They adored your generosity, your sense of fun and they delighted in your lightness of spirit. Your exuberance was a triumph against the bleakness of your childhood. You had turned to Kids Company social workers at your secondary school, plucked up the courage to ask for help.

Your mother lived in a mud hut fortified by corrugated iron sheets, a few chickens the sum of her worldly possessions. The poverty was jaw-dropping. Your two younger brothers could not go to school because there was no money. Their school fee was equivalent to half a business lunch at £50 per year. There was no running water; the toilet was dug deep into the earth. Your mother sent you to live with your father in England for a better life. There was no money for international calls and you lost touch with her. Your father married another woman, who resented your presence. Together they had a child, their family unit rendering you an outsider.

All your childhood you worked in your father's take-away shop after school, at weekends, and during the holidays, washing the floor and the dishes. Your work would continue all evening, until eleven or twelve o'clock and sometimes on into the morning.

Your father would not allow you any friends, your only contact with childhood was provided by the structure of school. You accepted your fate, resigned to this robbery of your youth. When you did not obey his rules, he humiliated you, called you fat and crooked. He beat you with sticks and belts, and your step-mother stood by watching. The humiliation and the shame were more painful than the lashes. You had no one to turn to but you did have similarly vulnerable friends at school. Together you shared secrets about the loss of your childhoods, accepted with resignation the blows life had dealt you.

You had been in hospital for years plastered in a cast. They had broken your legs and had to reset them. You were not healing, maybe a part of you wished for your premature death. Your distorted legs and your accumulated weight would have been survivable, had it not been for the daily humiliation you were subjected to. Your father trespassed further. At night while you lay in bed, he gave himself permission to touch you inappropriately and as time went on it led to penetration. As you described his violation the tears draped down your rounded cheeks. I could not help but wipe them. So many years you had missed out on having a mother. Your friends had persuaded you to reveal your secret to a Kids Company worker, and you grasped your dignity in hand to ask for help.

We reported our concern to social services. Too burdened, they initially refused to take the case on. Our workers pursued the offices and eventually you were given one night's place of safety. It only lasted a night because they soon discovered that your Home Office papers had not been processed. In the eyes of the law you were an illegal immigrant, despite the fact that you had spent much of your childhood in this country.

Legislation had given them a loophole. They rejected you from their care and told you to go back to your father. We were shocked, stunned at their cruelty and lack of vigilance. We reminded the child protection department of their child protection duties. There was your younger brother still in the house. They owed him a duty of care as a British citizen. That vulnerable children should be subjected to such divisions is shocking in itself, especially when British mainstream politics prides itself on its compassion towards the children of Africa. We watched Live8 and marvelled at the hypocrisy.

They did a police investigation. Your father cleverly admitted to hitting you, but not to the abuse. As a sexual abuser he would have been on the sex offenders register for life. As a father who disciplined his children, albeit with a belt, he could be culturally expressing his love for his children. The social worker left you homeless and without money, you were not eligible for benefits. Who were you going to turn to?

When we saw the impasse we decided to house you ourselves. We were a children's charity with no statutory rights, no power to argue with social services or to challenge the inappropriateness of their decision. Social services in turn were powerless to change the immigration legislation. They could not argue with the Home Office.

An extraordinary couple gave you their children's bedroom and their youngsters slept in the living room. You lived in this tiny two bedroom flat, the three children of this couple. They showed you more love, more acceptance and more welcome than your blood father could have ever dreamt of.

The road to recovery was fractious. You were afraid, unsure of what to do when no parent, either corporate or blood, stood by you. Your step-mother called once to complain of your having spoiled your father's reputation, and then she called no more. Your father never contacted you or attempted to have you back. Maybe it was his way of protecting you from his inappropriate and damaging sexual behaviour, or maybe he had forgotten to love you.

Every day we paid for a taxi from North London to South London to enable you to attend your school. You were afraid of sitting on buses, too shocked, too disorientated.

You delighted in being a child again, having water fights in the garden, going round to your friends' houses to do each others' hair. You wanted to be taken to the park and to play with toys, all the things you had been denied. You even dared to strop, moan about stuff, and be told off for keeping your room untidy.

In your foster carers you found two committed and generous people. He was famous in the urban music business. He took you to gigs, introduced you to friends and felt proud of your developing confidence. He was everything a good father should have been. She spent time gently untangling the traumas of your life, her words soothing, her shock when she heard what you had been through affirming your right to expect a childhood.

At school your work flourished. You developed aspirations. You wanted to be a nurse and help children. We delighted in your happiness and enthusiasm, but all the time we were trying to work out a solution to your immigration status. Your father was completely uncooperative. He would not allow us to collect your clothes or your GCSE coursework. He would not give us any information about his having applied for your leave to stay, and as time went on we realized he had never tried to keep you in the country.

Your situation made a mockery of child protection procedures. So many children like you are brought into the country, used as domestic servants and then abused or discarded. Children who get tortured for not obeying. Children who get used in ritualistic rites of passage. Children who are perceived as carrying demons and who are punished, burnt and sometimes narrowly escape death. We saw children like this every day. In some cases we got enough evidence together and we were able to initiate prosecutions, others we just knew about, but we remained powerless to act as we did not have the evidence that would have ensured the children's safe and permanent removal from their abusers. All those children and you were only young and at the mercy of the adults around you. Why must vulnerable children pay the price of ill-fitting policy and legislature drawn up by politicians? And you, Flower, you had to pay a double price. You were denied protection with the added insult of being told to return to your abuser. Where was the Human Rights Act? How could a child like you access justice, when even legal aid was denied? You had no confidence, your self-esteem battered. Who were you to turn to? All these people who create these laws imagining the protection of children make one fundamental mistake, they never put themselves in the place of the vulnerable child. How is a young child going to access the knowledge and the resources to fight for her own right to be safe and honoured as a child?

As we competent adults struggled, the law seemed confused, so open to interpretation. It was hard to believe that a social work manager was able to return a vulnerable girl to a house where she would be abused and hit again. Your peers at school watched our every move. They knew your story and they had similar stories to tell. They wondered what we would do. Would we abandon you when the going got tougher like others had?

We had no choice but to trace your mother. Your lack of legal status was denying you access to the health services you needed. It would also prevent you from going to college and medical school. Eventually we found her. Your mother's story was tragic, but she shared a spirit similar to yours. Telephone calls across the divide made preparations for your safe return. We identified a school you could attend and we paid for the fees. We also made sure that you would have clothes and safety, even though you were returning home to abject poverty to live in a mud-hut fortified with corrugated iron. Yet your love for your mother remained intact, as did hers for you and it was important for you to have that most fundamental of resources in child-hood – the attachment to a carer who cares.

Your goodbye party was a lively event. Neighbours from all over the street who had shared in the story of your care arrived with gifts. To every one of them you had a special meaning. You represented the vulnerabilities of each one, and the possibility of human kindness embracing someone at times of need.

You baked the cake, provided lots of drinks, and we played your favourite music. None of us could have predicted what lay ahead. We took you to the airport and you bought childish comics to entertain yourself on the plane. We felt proud of the fact that our care had returned your will to live to you, and we were proud that we had found your mother, someone who would be able to love you. Your future seemed something you could look forward to.

Two days later the call came. Your mother rang to tell us that you had died. On the plane you had a diabetes attack, which subsequently developed into a diabetic coma from which you never woke up. No one knew you had diabetes.

At least your mother saw you on this last day and you were both united knowing the love you had for one another, and I was left cherishing a beautiful letter you had written to me before you left.

Your note thanked us for being your parents, for keeping you safe, for believing you, and above all for standing by all children.

What shocked me was that your father turned up at your funeral. Your mother knew what he had done but she was unable to speak out about it. Someone should at last have held him accountable for his actions, but there was a conspiratorial silence. We paid for your coffin and the plot of land in which you were buried. We watched you get buried, a victim of betrayal parading as justice. Your forgiveness was profoundly humbling.

A PLEA FOR WISDOM

The relationship between workers and clients

Immigration laws are failing vulnerable children. Asylum-seeking children and families cope with complex cultural as well as psychological challenges. Therapeutic and social work practitioners, relentlessly faced with their clients' distress, can sometimes resort to the same protective defence mechanisms as their clients, in order to self-preserve.

Sometimes the capacity to feel is extinguished. Through numbness the worker feels protected against helplessness and pain. Through shutting down the ability to feel, you no longer have the will to act, to bring about change.

Workers who are overwhelmed experience themselves as victims and may over-identify with the powerlessness of the client. This sustains a client in their vulnerability and paralyzes the practitioner's thinking. Both client and worker get stuck.

To justify a lack of action, the worker may resort to denial, not believing the client's story or trying to minimize its significance.

The client feels catastrophically humiliated and dropped out of the worker's mind, as if she is too toxic to be embraced.

Sometimes workers suffer from bystander guilt. They feel bad for not having been able to intervene in a situation and prevent the client from being harmed. They blame themselves for what they perceive to be their impotence.

Sometimes a worker can feel secretly happy when a particularly difficult client is harmed or attacked. They feel the attacker has acted vicariously for them, delivering a revenge they wished for but could not action.

The more vulnerable and depleted worker can feel jealous of the support the client is accessing. They may wish that the same efforts to help were galvanized in their direction. The sense of envy can be acted out destructively, depriving the client of the support in order to reduce the worker's resentment.

Sometimes clients do not show appreciation. They feel too ashamed to admit to using and needing the help they are given. The admission of vulnerability is too painful and shaming.

The client who recovers often wishes to forget the organization and the people who helped because to remember is to be reminded of how vulnerable they were.

Sometimes workers perceive their managers as cruel for not providing help to the client. They may perceive the management as the client perceives the perpetrator. In this way the worker and client become over-identified with each other as victims.

Workers who are not able to solve the client's problems or address their pain may feel de-skilled, rubbished and ashamed. The worker may unwittingly avoid the client, as coming face-to-face with them is a reminder of their mutual hopelessness.

Excessive demand on a worker may be depleting of their resources. When a client asks for help the worker then feels angry, as if too much is being taken from them.

Workers can feel like a glass too full of mourning and pain. A little stress may overspill the container, unleashing the exhaustion like a catastrophe.

Therapeutic workers may feel angry as they perceive the client to be wasting the opportunities provided for her. It is as if the client frustrates the workers' aspirations on their behalf. But the client may not be psychologically ready to take up chances. Sometimes the barriers are invisible.

At times clients appear as competent and capable. In reality they may be really frightened of trying new experiences.

Trauma can feel contagious. The worker may be affected vicariously as they take on board the extent of the cruelty expressed by the human race. A sense of despair and despondency may invade the worker.

There are times when the worker may become desensitized to pain. Their threshold for feelings of horror becomes higher, having been overexposed to horrific situations. In becoming too familiar with emotional pain, they may not register its impact on their client.

An impassive and unexpressive worker may unknowingly mimic the cruelty of a cold perpetrator, who watched as the victim was harmed and did not react or prevent the pain.

Lack of sympathy for the pain experienced by the client may make the individual feel diminished and ashamed in the eyes of the worker.

Yet workers who react excessively to their client's pain may take up too much of the emotional space. The client may feel she needs to "soften" what she says for fear of hurting the worker's feelings or damaging them.

Clients may be wary of the worker, fearing them to be too fragile to hear their story.

The recounting of traumatic stories and their "witnessing" by the worker can help the process of working through the shock experienced by the client.

Sometimes clients feel they have told workers too much. They may withdraw to regain a sense of composure. The worker must not feel let down or rejected.

In order to gain intimacy with one worker a client may discuss another worker negatively. In diminishing one worker's efforts the thought is that the other worker may feel elevated. And the hope is that, feeling elevated, the worker will like the client more.

Workers should not forget that they deserve to exercise their compassion and the dignity that goes with it, just as much as the client deserves to be at the receiving end of it.

CHAPTER 9

Parental Addiction

Letter to Julie

DEAR JULIE,

Specialness glows in your face. Your cheeks round and sunkissed, your eyes full of tender grace. You are only twenty, and yet all the other more troubled children turn to you like an older sister and a mother. Your little flat in Peckham is a haven for lonely and desperate children.

I marvel when you struggle to write your first cheque and chuckle to myself at the sense of responsibility driving you to prioritize your bills. I love the way you have organized yourself into a routine, going to bingo on Thursdays and food shopping with your nan on Saturdays. You look so beautiful, and when I think of your amazing gains, I remember from what a painful place they emerge. The memory stirs up tears.

I remember hearing of you as a nine-year-old in a school in South London. I was supervising your trainee therapist. She clearly cherished you, but her smile always cut short halfway as some worry would interrupt the delight she felt. We knew you had secrets, but you were too well guarded. You expressed real joy in the play room, touching every toy as if it was yours. But your desperation made us alert, and your therapist found your sadness heartbreaking as you left the session. A child with such composure, such dignity and a deeply burdened silence.

Years later you were to tell me that this was the age when your mother first offered you cannabis. I will never forget the sense of betrayal. I remember my concern at the time. I took my worrying to bed, pondered at night what it was you were so unable to tell.

You and your siblings suddenly disappeared and you didn't come to therapy again, like so many other vulnerable children you became a shifting statistic leaving one register, perhaps to reappear on another. More faceless, mindless trafficking of children from place to place.

Two years or so later when our children's centre opened at The Arches, you reappeared. I had never actually seen you, but I had never forgotten you and the description of your therapy sessions. You still seemed silent, vigilant and bewildered, you were still secretive. With you came your eight- and nine-year-old brothers as well as your five-year-old sister. Your feisty little family, beautiful glinting faces obscured by dirt. You were only a twelve-year-old, but the responsibility was palpable in every inch of your tense muscles. You disguised your own need and kept busy meeting the desires of your siblings. It was simple things they wanted: food, warmth and shoes.

Soon we discovered none of you were in school. After you had disappeared from your primary school as a ten-year-old, you had not gone back to school; neither had your brothers and sister. You kept bursting into tears, but we could not identify the origins of your pain. It was sad, sad to see so many official letters had been sent home, demanding your parents to send you to school. So many letters threatening them to be taken to court. But no human being had bothered to knock on the door and find out where four children had gone. You invisible children drifted to the streets, disappearing in the mayhem of Peckham. No one really knew your secrets.

Then my worries began escalating. Your younger brothers were ferociously teasing you. They had caught you having oral sex with the local older boys. Beautiful you, called a "slag", hunted down by the boys, forced into sexual favours. They were simultaneously disgusted and desperate, your little brothers. They wanted to protect you.

One dark night, as we sat together in the art room, your tears began rolling drip, drip off your precious face. The secret leaked through the cracks of your well-defended walls. Before you reached the age of seven, your parents were dealers of drugs and favours. They sent all you children to amusement parks and bought you presents.

You describe yourself as wanting for nothing. By the time you were seven, the domestic violence had escalated. Your father began his heroin habit and would lie vomiting and unconscious behind the toilet door. Soon after, your mother became addicted and both spent long hours in drug crazed stupors. Heroin, crack and the devastation of your idyllic space. They had done it for years. The ferocious hunger you all exhibited and your hoarding of food in bags and pockets was explained. But your particular story was more devastating, more rotten.

A few days after you had told me this, your mother claimed the washing machine had broken down, and because of it none of you could attend school, because she was unable to wash the school uniform. I had to laugh. No school uniform had been worn by you for years. She wanted money for a new machine and had sent you as a messenger. Your shame was obvious. You hung your head deep into your chest. You knew her request was a lie, but if you didn't deliver, in her drug withdrawal frenzy, she would have beaten you. I sensed your desperation and told you I would not help, unless I could come to the house.

When the door opened I wanted to cry. Four special children living in such depleted conditions. I knew you were forced to do the housework, but no amount of goodwill would have normalized your home. It was a drug den, the duvets black, dirty, the sofa scarred with burns. No toys. No comfort. No wonder you held on to the therapy room toys with such wistfulness. Your mother's gaze rolled away from mine. Humiliation and stupor could not meet my eyes. She was emaciated, gaunt, struggling to coordinate stick-like limbs. She too looked vulnerable.

She tried her talk and her charm, but I knew how cruel she could be. Kindly and gently I confronted her about her drugs use, and she robustly denied it. But every item of dying furniture told the history of debauchery in that house. All you children crowded into your bed for comfort and safety. And then you described how one day the police had burst in seeking drug dealers and in the frenzy that followed they had shot your dog, the blood splattered all over the walls and then dripped onto the floor.

She was not the mother. You were. You held ferocious standards of care, like a mother should have done, but at such a devastating cost to yourself, "sucking dicks for money" to feed all of you. And then you had to tolerate the further indignity of being teased about it. You made the sacrifices of a mother and they called you a whore.

I wrote to social services, my belly filled with alarm. You were all very unsafe in that cold and random space. Social services did not have enough money to listen. You were not being beaten in such a way that they could compile evidence. They wanted proof of your being at risk beyond your non-school attendance and your hunger. They were sarcastic in their letters to me. It was as if, unless you had severe physical damage, no evidence would have been good enough. Your case was not meeting their thresholds of intake. You could not be described as a child at risk because there were too many like you out there. They had to "gatekeep", only letting in those who had experienced sexual abuse and extreme physical harm. At the time I did not know about the secret thresholds. I kept knocking on the doors, pleading for help like a bird flying into a concrete wall.

Relentless letter-writing finally brought me and social services to the table and then I discovered they had notes describing you as a seven-year-old, scavenging in bins for food, a baby in your arms. It must have been one of your brothers.

They had reports of your then three-year-old sister swallowing your mother's methadone. The files were full of misery and your bleak history lodged like a wound in my heart.

Social services were not there when you stole food from shops to make bread, butter and crisp sandwiches. Your bellies rumbling from days of hunger. They were not there when your mother tried to burn your hand on the cooker as punishment or held a knife to your throat for not washing up. They were not there when your mother's drug dealer pushed his adult tongue down your little throat for his sexual gratification. They were not there when your father battered your mother and you had to call the police, aged seven. Where were they, when shivering with cold you pushed your little sister's pram across the desolate estate, because you were too terrified to go home.

When you stole money to buy sweets and hid them under the kitchen cabinet, she punished you, little hungry girl, by forcing you to watch the other children eat everything you had hoarded, sarcastically laughing at the cruelty she facilitated. You felt so much shame. The callousness of a mother and abuser merged, affording you no escape.

Your seven-year-old sister froze in terror, too. She had witnessed a drug addict thrown onto a concrete floor out of his apartment window – a punishment for unpaid debt. The man died and she lost her speech for days.

The social services' intervention was tokenistic. They agreed to send a social worker to the house because your mother had hit you in the street with her shoe, facilitating a bruise as evidence, which warranted the meeting of their thresholds for intervention. But your mother had already threatened you into silence. As the social worker took action and interviewed you in the house, your mother hovered outside the door, her little menacing footsteps a reminder of how you could be battered if you spoke. I felt so bad. I put you more at risk and helped solve none of your problems. I had such deep love for you. The memory of it still makes me choke. But I could not stop those silent tears dripping off your luminous and beautiful face. Sometimes you suppressed your cries so much, the gasping felt like it was strangling both our throats.

It was a dark night when the police phoned. Just before Christmas. You were in their custody and you had asked for me. They had held you in a cell, a twelve-year-old child, hoping to break your spirit and frighten you into confessing to your crime. It was your father they really wanted. He had taken you on a robbery in his car. Your job was to knock on the door to ask for a fictitious direction. If a householder opened the door, he would move on. If they didn't, he would break into the house and steal all that could fit in the boot of his car. You were often forced to be his accomplice.

He loved you, but he was not really your father. The real one, you only met for the first time when he was dying of cancer in prison years later. Despite being your biological father he betrayed you time and time again and you gave up any hope of being genuinely reunited with him. In the absence of your own father you were desperate to belong to this combined family unit. It was all you had. Your step-father cared for you all. He was a father in the love he had, so you wanted to believe. But deep, deep down you have never been sure. You have never been able to confront him for the way he used you. He was honest, describing himself as a heroin addict for ever.

How could you admit to having three rotten parental figures? You wanted one to be good, and the one you tried to keep in a positive light was your step-father. But he did not care to protect you. Both of you were destined for the police station. The police officer could hear the worry in my voice. I challenged him about keeping you overnight without legal representation and cried when you showed me the handcuff bruises on your little wrists. They dropped the case against you, but greater punishment awaited. Your step-father was given a lengthy prison sentence.

You and your drug-addicted mother were left with three vulnerable younger children. Who was going to support her habit now that her robbing husband was incarcerated? I know you would have preferred the four walls of a cell, compared to the hell you were exposed to next. Your mother began cajoling you into delivering sexual favours to men in return for money to feed your siblings and to support her addiction. You felt disgusted, but forced into meeting your family's basic needs. The sexual encounters made you feel dirty, contaminated and rotten. You gagged and choked as men penetrated your little mouth down to your throat. As they released to satisfaction, you felt creepingly sullied and a "whore".

One devastating day, a grown father of four children drove you to his house with your friend and raped you both. A thirteen- and a twelve-year-old. The terrorized glint in your eyes to this day tears into my soul. He was the local baker, his shop below your flat. What indignity. Every day you saw him, and were unable to deliver a retribution. He and his colleagues sniggered, as they knew that the police had dropped the case and that social services remained complacent, having gone through all the child protection procedures.

Your desperation and depression had reached a peak. Your little brothers, aware of the horrors, acted out with dangerous behaviour. They broke windows, climbed bridges and roofs and dangled their little legs in anticipation of suicide. But it was you who could take no more.

Fed up with the chaos generated by your household, the neighbours gathered momentum and had you all evicted from the flat. Everybody in a frenzy to protect their quality of life. Not one person giving thought to the absence of quality of life that you were exposed to. All of you, four children and your mother, ended up in your grandmother's one-bedroom flat. The situation was untenable and soon her neighbours galvanized to evict you all too, and she lost her flat. The antisocial behaviour brigade paraded their triumph at the expense of such vulnerable and desperate children.

Eventually the self-disgust was invasive. You felt banished and contaminated, dirty, unworthy and cheap. You criticized yourself, feeling more self-disgust than anyone else could have made you feel. You tolerated the merciless teasing and the insults. It was the "whore" and the "slut", as well as the tiny and tired thirteen-year-old you wanted to bury. You popped the killer pills in the hope of finding solace in death, and you wanted to die to put an end to your lack of hope.

You were spiritually and morally exhausted, you courageous little mother. Everything around you was breaking down and your efforts to keep your siblings protected were also bearing no fruit. As your brothers and sisters expressed their pain in bad behaviour, you felt you had failed on all fronts. You wanted to punish yourself and express your self-hate by dying. But something kept you alive long enough for the emergency services to deliver you to stomach pumping and charcoal. Your life was saved, but your self-destruction had just begun.

You increased your drug use to reduce the unbearable pain, and you watched as, by force, social services dragged your brothers and sister into foster care. You were separated. They were sent to the countryside and lived with a family in tremendous anticipation of care. But you, you ended up with foster carers from whom you ran away. One broken placement led to another.

You were filled with hope, as your new foster carer promised to be a good mother. Clean sheets, fruit and aspirations. You shared a room with another child and shared her maternal care with other foster children. You loved her, but you could not bear her maternal embrace. It was too painful to receive such care from a complete stranger. It was your mother you wanted.

You hoped that the shock of losing her children would prompt your mother to give up her addiction. Every day you looked for signs of progress, a fresher look, a bit more light in her dreary eyes, perhaps a bit more weight. And you watched with jealousy and pain as your foster carer and her biological daughter shared the mother–child relationship you had always wanted. You could not tolerate this half-space, this limbo of love, where you neither had a mother, nor could turn to the one you needed.

Eventually, you stole money from this foster carer, and you aroused her rage. She should have forgiven you. She should have stayed and stuck it out. She should have shown comprehension for the devastation you were experiencing. She should have understood your jealousy and your regret and your deeply, deeply painful yearning for your own mother. Instead, she slammed her doors in your face, and I watched you as you cried because yet again you were losing something that could have promised some joy and some feeling of care.

Eventually your home became the local children's home along with other vulnerable children like you. You listened to the clanking of keys every morning as the doors were opened and locked. The only piece of tenderness and genuine loving care came from the kitchen cleaner. She made cake and hugged you, while staff came and went filling in their charts and anticipating their rotas. The children's home manager had terrifyingly long nails which curled, in a reflection of her churlishness. There was no real love there. Efficiency and sanctions dominated the institution's philosophy, while the children were deprived and left with unmet needs, disguising their lack with threats and terror.

There was no warmth and all the time the children were punished for their misdemeanours by being deprived of their pocket money. The local drug dealers knew it. They knew the children in the children's home had nothing and they stood at the doors promising presents and happiness. In this way you ended up standing in the corners of King's Cross peddling drugs, crack cocaine and then you began taking it. The terrifying class A drugs, the crack, cocaine snorted up your nose, smoked through the foils. The crack pipe and you sat on the children's home bed, hopeless about tomorrow.

The craving was driving you crazy as your drug use escalated. And in order to feed your habit you now turned to prostitution. You slept with one man after another. The childhood trauma repeated over and over again. But your reactions, your tears, were all suppressed by the control the drugs had over you. The risks were terrorizing. You were battered, abused, locked up sometimes and often used. Some nights you had sex with lots of men, each one giving you more drugs, feeding your habit and robbing you of your dignity. You were terrified, scared to say no, so you opened your legs and hoped it would finish soon. You began looking bleary-eyed, distressed. You lied, you stole, you shoplifted. The love between us was intense, but even this love could not prevent you from stealing from me. You took my cashpoint card and you took money, and with the betrayal you devastated yourself. But I wasn't going to give up. I loved you too much and I knew how desperate you were.

We kept meeting at the children's home. The staff shifted their platitudes from file to file. At last I decided that we had to put you onto a rehab programme in order to stop you from being out of control. I was afraid. I was afraid you would die and I was afraid that your beautiful soul would never get the chance to thrive again.

I remember your being driven through the countryside. You had never seen sheep and it was the furthest you had gone away. There was panic in your voice on the phone. One of our workers drove you to a drug rehab unit for children, a space of tragedy. So many young children whose devastated lives had turned them to drug use as a solution and a pacifier. You were desperate there. Every night you kept ringing me crying, begging to come back. You were inconsolable. They could not help you and eventually they put you on the train back to us.

At least you were with people who loved you and who cherished you and that is really what you needed more than the rehabilitation. We worked together as you determinedly battled against your addiction. Eventually the children's home moved you into semi-independent accommodation in preparation for moving into your own flat. You were excited. It promised new beginnings, but in the midst of all this you had met a new boyfriend.

He loved you in his own way, but he was dangerous to you, having different relationships at the same time and being a drug dealer. At night he would go out, transporting his drugs in cling film in his mouth or hiding them somewhere in the neighbourhood for the recipient to collect. He would deliver his goods and then come back to your little flat hoping to have sex. You were trapped. He was violent and one night I received a desperate call from you, since he had smashed open a piece of your skull in the battering. Your head was bleeding and you had locked yourself in the flat. I had to call the police and the emergency services to try and reach you. You were sobbing hysterically on the phone, as if the end had come. And yet, despite all the suffering and desolation he was causing you, he was the only person you had.

You were becoming aware of your mother prostituting on the streets. Sometimes you had found her in drug dens or you heard from her friends who were also addicted that she had robbed one of them. As you watched her sleep with one damaged man after another, you endeavoured to protect her dignity and status as your mother. You described two men having sex with her. The scabs on one of their heads drove blood to trickle down to his face. The leaked blood had dried to a crust on his cheeks but he was too bleary-eyed to notice. His short and dirty bitten finger nails grabbed your mother's breast. You watched the sexualization of her motherhood.

She did not contact your brothers and sister in foster care. She forgot her motherhood, but you forged it for her, on birthday and Christmas cards to your siblings. You kept their hope and yours alive that one day your mother would be a mum.

So many times she disappointed you. One Christmas Day we gave you a teddy bear donated by Harrods. You were so excited as you embraced the bear with delight and disbelief. By Boxing Day your mother had sold it for drugs money. I remember you crying. What words of comfort could I offer to dilute your pain? Sometimes she wrote to you making promises. She would go into rehab, but take drugs in with her. She was hospitalized, battered, sometimes lost. Only once she apologized when you challenged her, but since then you have not seen her. She stole from you too.

It looked like you and your mother could not really be reunited and any hope of creating a family unit with her was dashed. In the meantime, your step-father came out of prison. You turned to him for a short while, in the hope that he would not re-offend and be incarcerated again. But he re-offended and let all of you down. The only person who came and stayed with you every night was your drug dealer boyfriend. And even though he slept with other girls and he battered you, he was still better than that devastating emptiness you tried to avoid every day.

I wish people could see your courage, as every day you battle against devastating loneliness. You plan your days, keeping busy, always creating milestones which can keep you hopeful. Shopping for food which can be stored, in memory of the long days you all went without in hunger. You help other children and their teenage mothers, putting plastic paddling-pools outside your flat balcony for the toddlers to kick about in. Your house is an oasis for so many vulnerable children who delight in your love and sense of fun. You gave up your class A drugs and occasionally use cannabis to calm your restless soul. Every day you fight to overcome the legacy of a shattered childhood.

People think it is easy, this urban childhood, but even in your little flat you were not safe. One day a group of young twelve- and fifteen-year-olds burst in with their machine guns – not toy weapons, but killer tools. They threatened you and you had to lie on the ground, helpless again. Their intention was terror and robbery. You were lucky these child-killers did not take your life. The distress cast a bleak shadow. You shivered with rage and injustice. No one could catch them. One trauma too many and your life was fragmented to pieces only for you to pick it up, morsel by morsel, struggling again against the despair.

Despite everything that has happened to you, you remain resilient, feisty, beautiful and truly amazing. They awarded you the Young Carer of the Year. You deserved the accolade for the courage you have shown all these years. I have seen commitment and standards of emotional excellence in you well beyond your years.

For your brothers and sisters you are a mother, a beacon of hope. The love and respect you deserve is boundless.

As I read this letter to you, tears rolled. You cried, feeling acknowledged, and you hugged me. "I love you", you whispered. There will never be words good enough to define your spirit. Thank you for being an inspiration. I struggled to keep back my tears too. The dam broke.

PLEA FOR WISDOM

Parental substance abuse and its impact on children

The children of substance abusers experience life as arbitrary, erratic and inconsistent. The child is hyper-vigilant, always watching out for danger, scanning for terror. Children may try to be invisible in order not to be at the receiving end of harm.

The substances the parent is addicted to assume an important identity within the family. The drugs may be experienced as more wanted, more loved and more favoured than the child. The child may be jealous of the special relationship between the parent and their substances. Sometimes they can feel left out.

With a sense of dread being omnipresent, the child may struggle to self-calm. It's not self-soothing if it doesn't lead to solace. The child may struggle to keep her sense of identity, as the act of survival completely consumes her thinking space.

Children of substance abusers may worry about becoming addicted themselves. They may be given drugs by their parents, sometimes even cannabis to stop them from crying as babies. Sometimes the child may succumb to using substances in the hope that this will create greater intimacy between her and her carers. It is as if she wants to share the experience of addiction with her mother or father as a form of being close and attached.

Children may be vulnerable as a result of dealers and other drug users who come to the house. There may be greater risk of sexual abuse at the hands of strangers as well as parents. The dealers may recruit the children to work for them as couriers. Dealers to the parents may later become dealers to the child. Children are often sent on errands to dangerous places, either to deliver money or to pick up drugs for the carer. Sometimes the dealers may be very kind to the child and the child may look forward to seeing them. Sometimes children may develop crushes on the dealers or be sexually attracted to them.

Children may be traumatized by what the parent looks like or how he or she behaves while under the influence, or while in a state of withdrawal. The erratic behaviour of parents and carers may create a sense of dread in the child. Terror is omnipresent and forces the child into either hyper-vigilance or a state of exhaustion.

Children of addicts are often missing the basic necessities like clothes, food and underwear. Their medical needs are also often denied, as the household is very chaotic. The child may feel exhausted as night-times are un-tranquil. They may not be able to sleep. The sheer worry of surviving the chaotic and frightening state of their households may reduce their physical resilience. Children may look tired with bags under their eyes. They may look gaunt and have a sense of energylessness. Lack of energy is often compounded by lack of food. Children may accidentally overdose on parents' drugs. They may be infected by HIV and other infections by coming into contact with drug paraphernalia.

Young people may feel stigmatized as the neighbourhood shares the knowledge about their parents' substance misuse. If prostitution is involved as a way of acquiring drugs, the children in the household may feel ashamed and highly protective towards their carers, while being teased by their peers. Any attack on the parent may provoke a rageful reaction. The child may simultaneously protect the carer while also hating them for putting them in a position of difficulty with peers.

Adults addicted to substances may create a sense of corrosive control. Children are often threatened into silence by their parent and forced to lie about life at home. They may not seek help or accept interventions from professionals because they fear their parent may be imprisoned or the children may be put into care.

Older children may be forced into parenting younger ones as the adults in the household are too preoccupied with meeting their own needs. This may lead to a sense of social rejection and isolation in the older child, who will not be able to be free of responsibility and join her peers in activities. Sometimes shortage of money or the right clothes may lead to the child self-excluding in order to spare themselves from a feeling of humiliation.

A sense of deep insecurity may remain with children who have grown up in households where the parent was a substance abuser. In adult life the offspring may hoard food or goods, or panic at not having money in their pockets, as if the lack of power may plunge them back into the desolate childhood from which they emerged.

The self-esteem of children living with substance abusers is fragile. They may have developed competencies, but they seem invariably to feel these are fake and that they are fundamentally a fraud. It is the sense of having a secret which creates this dual reality. The abusive experience seems to invade every aspect of life like a malignancy. Often children of drug users have to battle against depression and despair. Even their adult life may feel more like a "rehearsal" than a reality; the sense of reality remains distorted by their drug impacted childhood.

All care relationships and the capacity to trust may be disrupted. Parental rules may feel arbitrary, punishments cruel and sadistic. The drug-abusing parent creates a sense of catastrophic chaos.

The child may always live in the hope that someday the parent may give up his or her addiction. The waiting, hopefulness and disappointments can feel like an emotional rollercoaster. Often children worry about finding their parents dead. At times they mistake drug stupor for death.

Sometimes younger children are told by the addicted parent that the drugs are medicines and that the parent is sick. Children will spend years worrying about the parent's health and then the discovery that the substances are illegal and the parent is addicted may invoke a sense of rage and betrayal at having been lied to.

Children may compare their parent to non-drug-using parents. A sense of envy and wistfulness may develop, as they wait for their parent to behave like other mothers and fathers. It is often the simplest things that lead to a feeling of poignancy, for example, "mum cooking for me like mums should".

Children being abused at home often run away, putting themselves more at risk. Children of drug addicts often form an informal network of support, as they share similar secrets. They frequently lend each other clothes and food and give each other refuge when a parent is particularly out of control.

As adults, the sense of having been defeated by parental substance misuse may force the offspring to engage in relationships where they set about attempting to rescue other substance users. They seek to repair the trauma of powerlessness and to transform it into a resolution.

There is much a worker can learn from traumatized children: their sense of survival against the odds, their dignity and capacity to laugh. The magnitude and magnanimity of the emotions involved in their survival can make both therapeutic workers and children feel competent.

In order to create greater resilience in children who have been exposed to chronic neglect secondary to parental drug abuse, it is important to take into account their basic needs which are unmet, as these are often the most corrosive form of deprivation in their lives.

It is also the case that children who are addicted to substances and abuse them themselves often do not have access to appropriate rehabilitation programmes.

There are sometimes issues of separation as the parent is sent away to address his or her substance abuse and the children are left waiting for the parent to return. The cycle of apology and betrayal in itself can harden the children into a state of emotional numbness, as if they cannot bare disappointment again, so they do not dare to engage in belief when a parent promises recovery.

Children who survive traumatic events and inconsistencies, and continue embracing life, can teach us inspiration.

CHAPTER 10

Letter to Deny, Cry and Try

DEAREST DENY, CRY AND TRY,

You beautiful triplets expressed the three faces of your mother's madness and gifts.

At first I met you, Cry, your head hidden in your hoodie. Outsiders would have described you as a potential perpetrator. In fact, you were a victim, your violence only to yourself. So much shame held you to ransom in your tracksuit top. Peeping through your hideout were your almond shaped eyes, dewed with sorrow. You barely uttered a word as if shock had strangled your speech. Every so often, some fury would unleash and you would slam your head into the concrete wall, as if the thoughts, the terror and the despondency were too unbearable to be in your head.

You hated your skull. It had been squashed as the other two triplets vied with you for space inside your mother's womb. Your mother had also stamped on it with her foot. Numerous operations later, the true beauty of your face emerged and with it you tentatively allowed the sun to caress your skin. I witnessed how fearfully you permitted your head out of the hoodie. With the reduction in your sense of shame your speech flourished and we delighted in your capacity for poetry. Your wisdom, like an eerie piece of music, touched heart and mind with one stroke. This beautiful poem, our first insight into your world:

Squashed up for nine months
All three of us
You kept us warm, you fed us, you talked to us
We heard your sweet voice as we lay there in the dark
You pushed us out
Me then him
And six hours later you had the last
You gave us life, you watched us live
You watched us grow

We all turned to the tender age of eight
The age of experiments
The age of developments
Did I thrive? No
What did I learn? That I'm different
Why?
I don't know
But you showed me
I felt the pain, the hurt
I cried once, but no more
You don't see tears anymore
They stay within
Why do you love them and not me?
What did I do wrong?
You say I'm bad but I know I am not.
I want to go
I have to go, before you kill me
But I want to stay

Though I have gone you haven't changed
You still taunt me with your threats that enter my dreams
I'm all alone now, still wondering
Where did it all go wrong?

I'm sorry for what I did wrong
I'm sorry for being bad
I'm sorry for telling the police
I'm sorry for letting the family secret out
But most of all I'm sorry for believing you

For I am strong
And I am loveable
And I will succeed
For I am the greatest
And you can't touch me now

Your poetry and your glance swim into my being and I ache with the pain and brilliance you harbour. Your mother's womb gave you life and it also murdered you. Your utterances are pearled with wisdom, unassuming and profound. It's philosophy born of pain, of destitution, of loneliness twinning with contemplation.

Your mother struggled when you were three. She faked her own suicide, scattered the pills on the floor and called the police. The doctors recognized the plea for help and social services began their involvement.

At night, she would often party into the morning and leave you all alone. During the day, bleary-eyed, she would open the door for the care worker to take you all to nursery. You describe how sometimes you were so hungry that you would draw pictures of food on a piece of paper and then swallow it. When you were aged eight, exhausted and unable to care for you all, she sent you to Tobago. There the three of you were subjected to horrific sexual abuse and profoundly humiliated. You rarely spoke of this violation.

Aged twelve, you and Deny went on an exploratory adventure. Hours of walking from Waterloo brought you both to Regent Street and you chanced on the delights of Hamley's. You had never seen a toy shop before. Hours were spent playing in this excitement-exuding space, as you touched many a toy and rode up and down the escalators. Upon your return, your mother refused to let you back into the home. She left you hungry outside the door and told you to go back to Hamley's where you came from. The frostbite on your nose, the threat of abandonment tearing into your heart, and hours later, full of your pleading and crying, she was mobilized to open the door. You were hungry and asked her for food. A sudden and catastrophic fury was aroused and she attacked you on the stairs. Your brother Deny, to prevent her from harming you, punched her in the face. It is this incident which drove her to reject you both forever from the family home.

You described how, years later, aged eighteen, still vulnerable and profoundly in need, you both did the trip to Hamley's again. Some desire to complete a memory compelled you both to walk from Regent Street back to the old family home. You wanted to see your mother again. You wanted to knock on the door and have her open it. Maybe rewrite your life script. As you knocked, the neighbours blinked behind the net curtains, their curiosity peering through. Like years before, you kept knocking, hoping for a response. This time your mother had gone for good, unexpectedly. It was as if the pain repeated as you looked up at the building and you realized your family home was no more. She had accumulated her worldly possessions and gone on an around the world trip, disappearing to be found no more.

You talk of being strong and no longer ashamed, but the struggle remains, more profound and more deeply ingrained. For you the greater pain is the catastrophic feeling of emptiness. The lack of mother-love left you a desolation too unbearable to acknowledge. Sometimes the devastation is paralyzing. You hide under your duvet like a corpse in a coffin, finished with living, or regretting your birth. It is as if it was an error. For days this bleak enclosure cocoons and sustains your deadliness. How can I help you fill the never-ending chasm? The love you so deeply yearn for is not to be found. If your mother knew how she has tortured you.

One foster carer after another attempted to fill some of the void. The first carers, a religious couple in whose drawers you found voodoo dolls pierced with pins. Your stay with them terrifying and short. You had us to fight for you to persuade the social worker that an atmosphere of disturbance pervaded the home. From a mad mother delivered to the madness of another maternal carer.

In between multiple foster carers, you spent time in a children's home. The staff were on automatic, clocking in and out their hours of duty with every arrival and departure repeating the children's experiences of rejection. Sometimes you went pleading outside your mother's door, begging for her love. She would not open the door. Her paranoia had projected its evil onto you. It must have hurt so deeply to be perceived as so vile in her eyes. Sometimes she let you in, but her deeply unhealthy ways drove you to the point of desperation and you emptied your horror onto the furniture, slammed your fists and skull into her impregnable wall. The pain so burning it could have scattered you in ashes.

As you battled with your emotional pain, you retained your dignity. You developed your ability. You tentatively learnt to read and struggled to form the letters of the alphabet. Your speech raced ahead in its fluency. So cruel the discrepancy between your awe-inspiring intelligence and your problems with handwriting.

Today you are filled with sorrow, as you realize your education was so unfulfilled. Social services refused to pay for you to complete your learning. Constant moves from one foster carer to another prevented you from acquiring any GCSEs. And yet you want to go to university. You want to learn but if you are in full-time education, you risk losing your local authority flat and your benefits. You laugh with sarcasm at the Catch 22 that is created.

A caring foster mother eventually emerged. She and her family embraced you with acceptance. You had a room, a genuine source of warmth, but you hurt her. Her love was unbearable. You perceived it in the wrong mother. It was your biological parent whose tenderness you sought. Instead, a complete stranger endeavoured to mother you. The paradox drove you crazy. The more love you received from your foster carer, the more your heart ached for your own mother.

You describe how you left the gas on in the hope that her fury would be aroused and she would begin to behave with the same cruelty as your mother. You cleverly state how in the short term that would have reassured you, but in the long term you would have been terrified and unable to learn that some people could deal with you without fury or rejection. This foster carer's love tortured you – the kindness was agony. Every day, you struggled to live with what you perceived to be fate's cruel joke. Now you speak of how you attempted to destroy love for fear it would be withdrawn. You talk of how much confusion this ambivalent mother relationship has created with any girlfriends seeking intimacy. You are an emotional yo-yo, seeking proximity and recoiling into rejection.

In preparation for your leaving, the foster carer spoke of the impending separation. She had to process you out of her house. The care conveyor belt had declared the end of your childhood at sixteen. She rapidly endeavoured to teach you budgeting and independence, in the hope that you would survive living on your own.

You did not want to eat. The more you starved yourself, the more you came close to your biological mother's expression of her mother-hood. In the hunger you met her again, as she had deprived you of food for long periods. Sometimes to summon her essence, you would allow your little room to turn into a dirty, cluttered and chaotic space – the home of your childhood, as if the mess was her mothering and a reminder.

The desperation, the impending separation, conspired, drove you crazy, and you wanted to bring the madness to an end. You took her keys and drove her car into a wall, hoping to embrace your death and in the void achieve the tranquillity you had yearned for from your birth. Your survival from this suicide attempt delivered you to a male foster carer, a kind but distant man, who could not understand the complexity of your thinking, the intricate weave of your emotional fabric. He took away his house keys in acknowledgement of the place-ment failure.

Each time you perceived yourself as damaging your placements, you were filled with remorse and sadness. You could only tolerate the goodness of people who had cared for you in looking back on it.

Sometimes, the carer would be demonized, as if she or he har-boured monstrous intentions and thoughts. Even I battled against your rubbishing, as if you could not register my love for you. You would play social services up, setting them in the position of rescuer alongside against your perception of me as a threat. I pleaded with the senior manager not to collude with your disturbance. You needed help to hold on to the good, not to acquire allies in the polarization. But the senior manager was weary, tired, preoccupied with the politics of "rights" and not aware of how she had become a puppet in your game.

When the madness of confused perceptions and identity subsided, when the demonized mother was allowed to be dormant, and you could see me for who I was, you sat with me laughing, relieved that unlike all the other mother figures, I had not run away or been demolished by your hate. You had no tolerance for the emotional embrace of a stranger. It was your mother's arms you wanted.

Your yearning coloured your relationship with the other two triplets. Try had the most complicated position. He was the child your mother had chosen to keep, while she rejected you and your other brother. Two of her babies she discarded and the third she kept. You were never able to comprehend her choice. Perhaps it was possible that the child she kept was from a different man's sperm, and the two of you shared a father for whom she felt hatred.

Sometimes you explained that maybe your mother could not bare your emotions, your painful yearning for her love. You waiting in her maternal waiting room for the arrival of her motherhood. When you were in the children's home, she would buy Deny trainers and gifts but you nothing. You thought she liked the torturing and your begging and your desperation. The children's home workers insisted that she had to bring you a similar gift. Her response was never to visit again.

The cycle of pleading and begging and then being rejected continued with your mother, until in the end, she packed her bags and went. But months before her departure you and she had a meeting together. You took the initiative. You were the grown-up and when you arrived at the café where you were to meet, you decided that you would buy her the muffins and drink. She had no money. Even in this last visit, she was unable to be the parent. You sat with her, asked a question and then you laughed at how childlike she was. You said to me, "She was a silly little girl who had children and did her best, as silly little girls do". You felt sorry for her and you thought that perhaps you would be able to close this painful book. That your yearning would stop. That you would be able to find some peace, some resolution.

Right now, you live in your bedsit flat, struggling against your own self-destruction. Sometimes you are hopeful and have aspirations. You feel you can turn your pain creatively into something which can benefit others. You attempt to educate social services about providing a better facility for abandoned children. You join the local authority's board of "corporate parenting" and then laugh at the fact that they cancel every meeting. You have wisdom and the profound understanding pain has gifted you. You want to prevent other children from being similarly hurt by an emotionally clumsy system. You represent your peers at a youth parliament and you summon up all your psychological resources to sustain your participation in living.

At other times, you are vulnerable, susceptible to the recruitment of perverse Islamic brothers who prey on the emotionally empty belly of young people. They promise fulfilment through Allah and retribution. But even in this complicated space you manage to find some truth. You realize that your religion is like a mother – abstract, always available, a resource you can draw upon.

In recognition of your vulnerability, a firm of interior decorators embraces you, offering work placement and love. They are patient, appreciative of your specialness and they know how you struggle to hang on to a will to live. Every day you are brave, dignified and extraordinary. Every day you generate light, when bleakness could bring death to you. I do not know if I could invent my being every moment, the way you have to do to avoid the void. How much energy you use to keep alive, when meaninglessness could instantly erase. Your being full of poetry, more profound than the anthology of those who peddle emotions. You live life, every aware and painful moment of it gifted in finding hope.

When I read this letter to you, you sat in silence and then you told me that it was beautiful and true.

But your story goes beyond just yourself. There are your two triplet brothers. The cruelty finds expression at any given time, when any two of you triplets conspire against the third. Often it is Try who becomes the victim. He is perceived as having been with the biological mother when the two of you were abandoned. You think he had her love. His experience is different. He negotiated her madness and the unwelcome attention of her destructive friends. He turned the key in her door, not knowing if today he was the enemy or the friend. He battled against your jealousies and your resentment. I also gave a letter to him, but he was too mindful of your mother's feelings to want it included in the book. He thanked me and wanted a copy, saying, "It touched and broke my heart at the same time".

The story he tells is very similar, except that he was more able to forgive your mother. He recognized her murderous motherhood and yet wanted me to know that she was also a "super mum", holding down several jobs and wanting to better herself.

He too struggles with catastrophic emptiness. To Deny my letter turns.

DEAR DENY,

You have the dignity of a lion king, your speech more eloquent than the elocutioned. You think deep and feel a pain so profound, yet your face is still. You describe your emotions as if they were part of a computer program. You are polite and courteous, but you are not there. It feels as if you have packaged yourself for perfect presentation, but you are gone. The only time your self-control shatters is when you lose your temper, and then the most tempestuous storm is unleashed, lashing its rage against the walls and furnishings. You become ferocious, propelled into a killer state, the victim lucky to survive your claws.

You do not want to hurt anyone. You are constructive, kind, a trainee youth consultant contributing to strategic thinking. You are articulate, intelligent and in possession of great charm.

The storm brewing your spirit into terror is the product of your having been so profoundly violated. You are one of three triplets. Your mother you describe as pursuing the youth she had lost, and you remember having immense hate for her. You recall how she used to hit you with belts, slippers and her fists. She would berate you for being born and complain about the fact that your existence resulted in her not being able to realize her potential. She used to lock the kitchen door and the house, trapping you three and your primary school-age sister in the house. You were hungry, battered and the neighbours knew it. But no one mobilized to help.

I held back my tears as you described with unbearable pain how one of her friends, knowing of the abuse, used to put food through the letter box when your mother had abandoned you to the night. You four little children, glad to be receiving every morsel of cupcake which used to fall to the ground through the tiny metal flap in the door.

Your disturbed relationship with food continued. You would not eat and even now you are underweight. You describe how in the children's home the cook, angry at your rejection of her food, put rat poison into the dish. The prompt action of the manager prevented you from swallowing her killer meal. You went on at sixteen to train in a kitchen and the chef would hurl racist insults, saying how if he did not take the food out of the oven, it would become as black as you.

As a toddler your mother's cancer delivered you to a children's home in Kent. We laugh as you described mistaking the horse shit for Weetabix. The swans kept snapping at your little fingers and you could recollect breaking the eggs in the pigeon enclosure. You got sugar poisoning when you swallowed a whole bag of sugar and milk out of hunger. Never having seen a fire extinguisher, you flooded the carpets. This is the only truly happy recollection you have.

By age eleven, your mother had met Tammy. After one hour's meeting the three triplet children were flown to her house in Tobago. No one knew that Tammy was a child abuser and that even in this developing country with limited child protection structures, her children had been removed from her care. Yet your mother delivered you to her maternal space after one hour's encounter. Tammy hit you with belts, locked all of you in your room and then would withdraw one of you at a time into a claustrophobic enclosure where you were battered by her. You recollect your brother's screams as his genitals were pulled, dragging him across the floor. You describe with sadness too unbearable how you could not help him as you were locked up in the room next door. The screams echoed round and round in your head. You knew how much it hurt. You knew of the humiliation. You knew because it had happened to you too. This random picking of her victims. This was not your first experience of abuse. It had happened to you before with a relative, when you were six years old. All you can remember is the light flooding in from underneath the door. Now when you see light under the door, you are flooded with past feelings and fear. This unbearable invasion of your childhood.

You describe a constant state of terror. You have the memory of it now still in every cell. The hypervigilance, the fright beyond description. When you were about to leave school each day for Tammy's home you were so frightened you would lose control of your bodily functions. Standing up, your peers would tease you about having soiled your seat with faeces, your bowels evacuating the horror for which you had no words. So much humiliation.

Your thirteen-year-old sister watched you being battered and commented cruelly, suggesting you deserved it. When Tammy came to England and you stole her beating belt, your mother provided her with your grandmother's. You describe graphically how your grandmother's belt hurt even more, as it had pieces of metal attached to it. They dug into your flesh.

You do not need speech. I understand your silence. Every blow is stored, lash by lash, on your skin, in the depths of your body tissue. The cells hold the history, the fury, the shame, the terror; every micro-memory lodged inescapably into the fabric of your being.

How do you verbalize such pain? How do you not kill yourself after the event, chased by the ghost of it every walking and courageous moment of your existence? I feel your dignity, your weary resignation, and I hold back enough crying for both of us.

You tell me your suicide note is already written and you want me to include it in my letter. Here it is. Your way of saying what it takes to be alive every day.

Deny's suicide note

To whom it may concern

I am sorry to say, I'm going to give up. I cannot take it any more. I am in overwhelming pain and I have tried to stop it hurting. I can do it no more.

I'm going to try and make you understand where I'm coming from. My mum has done a lot of things that I have only just started to deal with. It started when I was about between four and five years old. She kept telling me to get out of her house and she kept on putting me outside. I always went to the nearby park with my favourite blanket. She would come to get me when she was ready.

At the age of six years old, I was abused by my godfather. He was my uncle's baby mother's brother. Ever since, I have been holding all of this inside me. So far, that is my foundation.

My first primary school was R—— school. My mother used to starve me, so I had to steal and eat other people's packed lunches. I bet you're wondering what happens next. Well, I was put into care and then I went back home. Then I was put into care after a while and I went back home. My anger started growing. All of this was before I was nine.

At nine, I had been through two primary schools and my third and last primary school. I got excluded. Almost every time I came back off an exclusion. My mother then decided that I was to have my education in Tobago. Once again, she left me to fend for myself.

It gets worse. She left me with a woman called Tammy, who abused me. For example, she would fling bottles, put her hand on anything she could get her hands on. She used to torture us. I needed to protect my brothers and to do so, I needed to fight her back. So I got more pain and abuse for my insolence.

At ten years old, I was at war with the beast and I was losing. I slept with a knife under my pillow, wishing it was a bad dream and hope tomorrow would not be as bad as yesterday, being woken up by a belt strap.

Eventually, the British Embassy got us home. Our mother met us at the airport. She sat us down and stated: "I have moved on with my life and I don't want you pulling me back." I listened to that, after the trauma me and my brothers had just been put through. We told mum what had happened. She did not believe us, saying, "Why didn't you tell me before?" I told her that Tammy stood over the phone as we spoke. I had made her my sworn enemy and I declared war on my mother. She said, when I was very able to confront her without being violent that she knew something was wrong.

But wait, why did she send my sister to investigate? My sister was loving the sun too much to care. She was only thirteen my sister. She was my mother's right-hand woman after this. Why she thought something was wrong, she did not come herself? Maybe she was telling the truth when she said that she made it all happen. You see, when I was in Tobago I saw Tammy's kids, who told me their mother was only allowed to see them once a year for a set time.

My sister played the mother role at times. My mother became scared of me and made my brothers slightly envious. I never saw my mum as a mother. From a little boy I called her "Yvonne" and then "Mum" when she told me to. She now calls herself Jazz. And the local education authority (LEA) could not be bothered, so my mother went to the BBC and asked for help. The LEA put me in a special needs school.

One night me and my brother came back from going out. She told my brother that he was not eating nothing. I guess it was the last straw for my brother. He called her a bitch. She got angry. She started to violently hit and stamp on his head. And that's when Tobago came to mind. Remember, I am still at war with her. So I punched her in the head to get her off him. She told us to leave and once again, I was in care.

At last, I hit college. At first I didn't want to go, because of my past. My foster mum encouraged me to go. So I went to college and I enrolled on a catering course. I was happy.

Four months into my course, a guy called Steve started to be racist. Example was "you kitchen monkey", and "you don't want it coming out like Deny", which damaged me mentally. I complained over five times. At sixteen, I was on antidepressants and broken. I was getting abuse from my foster parent and the chef matre. I was excluded for grabbing Steven and saying I was going to kill him. Thankfully, because I complained more than five times, I was let back, but not to the same campus. I went to another campus, but due to being from the previous campus I was not welcomed. I tried hard.

It was difficult and I was not prepared to work under such conditions, especially when I was the victim. I left college without qualifications, just mental scars. I, Deny, was nothing and a no one. A friend put me in touch with a restaurant. I worked for Alan on the weekends. He told me that I was good, and I should go to another college. I enrolled and I still can't get over what happened, no matter how hard I try. All that work I did, I had to do it over again, and it hurt and upset me. I cannot do it. I'm currently attending college doing professional chef's diploma. I regret to inform you that I will not complete the course due to my instability and low confidence.

Isn't it funny how something is so positive and it takes one little thing to turn into a negative. After an advanced personal development programme, I have been trying even harder. Please help me to move on, because I cannot go on like this.

Weapons down for this soldier of misfortune.

I have given up on life and catering. Slowly, not wanting to get up any more or do anything. If you're reading this, I may be dead or think that you can help me turn it around.

Thank you and goodbye.

When you told your mother about Tammy's beatings in Tobago, she remarked, "You should have used the tickets to come back". When you told her you didn't know there were any tickets, she remarked, "You should have known".

You recollect that by age twelve, you were strong enough to retaliate. If she beat you, then you beat her. You became powerful and discovered the true strength of violence for your protection and status. In the space of three years, you were placed with one foster carer who slammed your head into the wall; one who starved you of food (and whose own child refused to come to the house to see him); another who had a mansion but gave the children mouldy bread; a children's home where the worker got sacked for hurling you numerous times on the bed and getting on top of you with his army build; and one kind carer whose house you had to leave because her relatives were not police checked.

You graphically described how one children's home received you as a terrified young boy and then, a number of fights later, rendered you into an "alpha male". The power hierarchy in the children's home created a pecking order. You were initially numbered 2, number 1 just got shot. He was the most violent child but he was more just than any adult you had come across. He protected the children in the home. If someone upset them in the park or on the street, he would stab them. For much of your childhood, you slept with a knife under your pillow just in case you needed to use it too.

You felt ashamed of being in the children's home where everyone knew you had no home and no parent where you were wanted. Even your friends had to sign in like the workers who came and went. The endless agency staff told the amusement arcade you were children in care, shaming you all even on a fun trip. Yet you loved the manager and appreciated the thoughtful way she spoke to you, her respect for your safe status. Sometimes you would go back to visit her. You helped to bring her shopping back into the home from the car. There was also a man you liked, who shared the story of his life with you, and saw you, not as a beast, but a child in need. It feels as if the good mother is still missing. You go sometimes looking for her, but the rejection is painful. The foster carer you like told you not to come to the house unless you rang her before. You felt hurt and never went back.

You describe how often you hate women, their silly games, and yet you wait for a girlfriend who can understand. You are so fragile, despite the illusion of power. Your past and present separated by a fragile membrane, every painful memory permeates and impacts your perceptions now. The man who discloses sexual abuse at college turns your belly in recognition – the pain propelling you back to the abuse you survived – or maybe you didn't. You get embroiled in abuse of your need for nourishment then and you starve yourself while playing the chef.

As our conversations end, you ask me what you should do about your washing machine. In your fury, you broke the double glazed door to smithereens, along with punching in the walls and breaking all your plates. You are saddened, baffled by your own anger. Your flat mate is terrified, seeking answers for this catastrophic expression of your spirit. You hold back your tears, blink your eyes in resistance, but I can feel your desolation. I'm speechless. The paralyzing moment between us propels you into action. You're planning your next survival strategy, your next living task, helping you to embrace life and not death. You tell me if you had to rewrite your suicide note, it would end:

> I'm still here. It will take more than that to keep me down, for I am the deepest there is, profound respect and deep reflection into self truths. I know I can, I know I will, I know I'm going to. My inner truth for me is a part of my state of mind and determines my strategy. My planning of goals makes me strive to accomplish. Respectfully yours, Deny.

I marvel at your resilience, your capacity to keep going; your lion-like dignity and your natural leadership. However I ache for you. When I read this letter to you, your response was: "I felt the tears for a minute and then I shut down".

PLEA FOR WISDOM

Children experience circumstances differently. Even though the facts may be similar, it is important to listen to the child's perception of events, rather than superimpose your own reactions based on cold facts.

The family is like an intricate and complicated system, every member acquires a position and identity coloured by their relationship to carers and siblings. To understand the child's behaviour, we need to understand their relationship and functions within the system.

Children who have experienced maternal deprivation or catastrophic failure in care retain the feeling of desolation and emptiness. They may require assistance well into their adult life, to create a home and to have the capacity to self-soothe. Often they're suicidal. Suicide is a way out and must not be seen as entirely negative. The child needs to know that for them it is an option if they feel there is no possibility to recover or repair. In this way, the child has a sense of freedom. They do not feel trapped in their circumstances, and they understand that they do have the power to end. At the same time it is essential that every encouragement is given to the child so that they can share their suicidal thoughts and discuss them without shame or denial. The worker needs to encourage the child to find things for which they want to live and to be honest about the fact that the child may be feeling catastrophically empty and that they may need to find different things at different periods in their lives which make living worth engaging in. When the child has carefully planned a suicide attempt, then his concerns must be explored even more robustly in order to prevent its carrying out.

Children will act out dramas of the past within the relationships of the present. Sometimes the walls separating now and then are thin and fragile. The child may need to untangle perceptions, and the new carer requires support to survive the transference.

Children's homes can become, unwittingly, emotionally dangerous places, where violence, insecurity and lack of love can compromise the child's care. Workers must make every effort to be vigilant about the emotional climate of the house as well and its practical demands and duties.

Physical abuse is stored as physically engaged body memories. These experiences of violation can be unleashed in terrifyingly aggressive outbursts. The child often has little control and will need help to come to terms with the damage they have caused as well as with their extraordinary expression of violence.

Siblings in abusive situations often victimize each other. They may have thoughts that the other children had it easier. It is helpful to help them to see each other's experiences of events and allow for a respectful sharing and acceptance of different perceptions of the same situation.

The story of Deny, Cry and Try illustrates how the same three young boys had similar experiences of their mother, but different reactions to the events. It also illustrates what position each child adopted in relation to the others. Deny was always in the position of protecting Cry. Cry verbalized the abuse and the missing of his mother much more than the other boys. Deny survived much of the time not admitting that he was desperately missing his mother. And Try has attempted to make the best of the situation and he has achieved this by forgiving his mother. All three boys asked me to read their letters to all of them. This has helped deepen their relationships.

Conclusion

I STRUGGLED TO conclude this book. The process of writing it was much more painful than I had anticipated. When I read the letters to each child for their approval, something profound happened between us. They were deeply moved, as if for the first time their story was told with the emotional significance it deserved. Most of the children cried quietly. I did too.

They made no changes to their letters except on minor factual information. I checked carefully with them the implications of making their stories public and the potential impact on their parents and siblings. I was worried about making them feel ashamed or exploited. None of them wanted to withdraw the letters, except one child who was worried about his own safety in relation to his mother's contacts. After hearing the letters read to them, most of the young people made significant positive shifts in their lives. They kept saying a weight had lifted off their shoulders. What they needed was compassionate witnessing. However, we have to ask why these children would want you, complete strangers, to know their stories.

I think it may be about truth; about setting the record straight; about restoring to them a right to dignity. It's about justice. These children are often described in our public communications as menaces to society. We pride ourselves on the strategies we put in place to control them. So many of our current interventions with vulnerable children come from the perspective of the well-adjusted adult, needing to preserve our own sense of safety. Onto these fragile and marginalized children and families, we project our hate, and we disguise our revenge as legitimate punishment.

I understand why the public feels bullied by young people high on drugs and their own suicidal non-caring. The sense of injustice they subject us to is infuriating, terrifying, indeed terrorizing. But our encounters with these horrors are momentary and accidental, sometimes on the bus, on a train and often because we happen to be in the wrong place at the wrong time. It is unjust, and the anger builds up.

Imagine if the same bullying and terrorizing relentlessly happened in your own home by the people who were supposed to love and protect you. Imagine trying to work out why your mother abuses and your father neglects. Imagine being a child, helpless, subjected to humiliation, trapped behind closed doors. You take the abuse with no one to turn to. It's a dark existence with depleted aspirations. It is unjust, and the anger builds up.

The adults are angry and seeking revenge. The children are angry and acting revenge fully. It is a cycle of hate that needs to be interrupted. The regurgitation of horror stories in which adults are victims of out-of-control children is not achieving a resolution. Television programmes in which the teenage and toddler terrors are tamed by miracle workers are facile. The truth requires the telling.

I hope these letters will show you how special these children are. They are extraordinary in their courage. Every day they battle against catastrophic fragmentation. So often they feel emotionally empty – the void could paralyze them into inertia.

Imagine the strength it takes to see yourself through the day when suicide is so on call. How do you find meaning in living when meaninglessness seems so real? How do you define yourself when your existence feels obliterated by other people's hate? How do you greet people when you expect them to dislike you? It is so hard to meet someone's gaze when you feel so intrinsically flawed. How do you imagine yourself into the future when your belly is full of foreboding and you feel your living today is because death missed you by chance? Where do you find trust, when betrayal cynically shadows it? These are some of the psychological legacies of emotionally rotten childhoods.

Children physically terrorized describe other annihilating horrors. The body stores the blows, holds the score, and remembers the sores.

Children left to manage their bleeding vagina and anus after unwanted penetration. Children choking with adult needs for sexual gratification. Rage and reactions combine – fury waiting for expulsion. Horrors of physical abuse never fade. The memory is played back in flashbacks; time and time again the terror relentlessly repeating, now as if then. In children who have been abused there is the urge for revenge. The hate is outward-bound towards the victim and/or inward-directed towards the self. It is the expression of murdered childhoods.

We understand that those who harm their children have always been harmed. The cycle of intergenerational hate plays back its sick drama, reclaiming new victims. But are we aware of our own perverse roles as bystanders?

Our response is to trap disturbed children and their victims in photographs for our newspapers. Television programmes pursue teenagers in hoodies, seeking a trophy to illustrate urban warfare. At dinner parties, chattering teeth do the rounds of horror stories and, as if exposed to thrillers, we shrink into our chairs, relieved it wasn't us. The truth is, every one of us is responsible for the social fragmentation, for the escalation of violence, for the disrespect; for shattered childhoods. It's a systemic problem.

As usual, childlike wisdom has intelligence. These young people courageously took the first step in truth telling. They share with you their life stories so that your two-dimensional picture can acquire more depth. No child is born a criminal or a killer – something happens to generate hate in them.

I hope every adult reading this book will recognize their contribution to the neglect. It's about our refusal as a society to protect and honour childhood. When the child's parents abused and humiliated, we were not there to stop it. When the child turned to us for help, our services were under-resourced, often emotionally thoughtless and unwittingly repeating the abuse again. Too many abandoned children have been and are left to fend for themselves, like scavenging dogs fighting for morsels of professional intervention. Our contribution to this abuse is our complacency, our facile arguments, our pseudo-debates, our cosmetic short-term initiatives, our offensive neutrality, our readiness to perceive ourselves as victims, denying the children's damage.

Our arguments are bizarre. We believe disturbed behaviour in children is about the child being selfish and making poor moral choices. Yet science is demonstrating that neglected and abused children do not have the brain chemistry to make appropriate pro-social decisions. The neurobiological tools for thoughtful choice are damaged as a result of adult thoughtlessness. Yet, we point the finger of blame and watch the child like a trapped circus animal fail to perform to our expectations.

The child is disturbed. What is our excuse? We the professional, the city director, the media-wise communicator, the all-promising politician. Where are we hiding our disturbance? I suggest it may be hidden in our failure to take responsibility. We avoid our individual and corporate parenting tasks, our moral and emotional duty as adults, and in doing so fail our children. We are competitive with our own kids, narcissistically refusing to grow up. We want our own prolonged childhoods, with the choice to have it all. It's not children who steal our comfort; we have long stolen their emotional space. We have control over the resources and national communication networks. We set the agenda. We control the laws, and we want it all to ourselves in the service of our own needs and perceptions. Adult self-gratification is harming children and creating ghettos to which the marginalized are condemned.

I'm not advocating suffering to absolve guilt. I don't seek punishment and mindless self-sacrifice. Maybe we need to learn from the example of these children. The conditions are not good. The resources are limited. There is emptiness. But honesty could make the difference between dignified acceptance or being driven crazy. As adults we owe these children the truth. We are letting them down. Where we can prevent or reduce the damage, we must take responsibility and action. Where we are powerless, then we must empower the child with the integrity of our acknowledgement. With apology we are able to place the responsibility for the failure with us; and not avoid it by blaming the vulnerable child. The truth empowers people, restores to them their sanity and their dignity. Truth upholds justice for these children and for us.

The young people wanted to share with you their life stories in the service of honesty. It's not about feeling sorry for them. It's about our collective agony. It's an alarm to prevent the erosion of quality. It's about preserving our humanity. The truth is precious. It has energy and, despite the depletion, it bears gifts.

I have wondered about these children's sense of profound poetry. Their eloquence, their charm, their extraordinary dignity despite so much damage. How do they manage to keep their spirits so special? I feel lucky and privileged to be working with them. I love their honesty in hate and in love. They are not flawed. They simply reflect back our own social and emotional flaws. The witnessing hurts but when you find the courage to face their statements, the truth of it is liberating.

As a society, we have become diffident of being individually effective. We hide behind the comforting belief that the task is beyond us, that one individual cannot make a significant difference. Sometimes our sense of personal shame conspires to neutralize passionate aspirations, rendering them mediocre. We are afraid when others show care, when they stand up for something valuable. We mistake homogeny for efficiency and force our services to lose the brilliant contribution of those who are kind. The committed individual is perceived as too involved, as if feeling is somehow an indicator of incompetence, of inferiority or weakness.

Our structures are failing children because we're scared of love. The expression of our humanity terrifies us into political cowardice. We hide, we avoid, we minimize the truth and as a group we deaden the space where creative solutions could thrive. So often those in power are too busy minding their own professional backs and personal credit rating. On the way up they trample over the disenfranchised.

We need, as individuals, to reclaim our portion of the action, to make a personal difference. The excellence is in the detail. It is in the middle space where one person's care and the other's need mutually transforms. The special moments are when the children show emotion –

and yours and mine are enlivened. Children need our protection, and they need our love.

It leaves me to thank all the courageous children who have contributed to the spirit of this book. I hope as adults we will learn to honour your trust. I began as an attempt to set the record straight, to make justice visible, and I must end with our apology for the wrongs.

You collectively told the truth when we dared not.

The Basic "Who's Who?"
of the Therapy World

IN THIS SECTION I briefly identify types of therapeutic worker and the training they receive. There is always some overlap between what these people do. There is also a tendency for each group of professionals to focus on a certain area or aspect of thinking, depending on their training and their role in relation to the client.

Counsellors

Counsellors are people who have a capacity for care and understanding and who wish to train in supporting and doing therapeutic work with clients. Counsellors aim to help people overcome the emotional barriers or psychological problems caused by specific life issues, for example, stress, relationship breakdown, traumas, lack of self-confidence and addictions. Counselling enables clients to address their problems and make the life changes needed to overcome these problems and improve their health and well-being. Counsellors tend to focus on talking to the client and reflecting back on the clients' concerns and issues in the hope that resolutions can be found through mutual thinking between counsellor and client. Counsellors' work lasts for a mutually agreed length of time. Some counselling may be short-term, some slightly longer depending on the types of problem and the client's wishes. Sessions are usually fifty minutes once a week. All practising counsellors in the UK are registered with the British Association of Counselling and Psychotherapy (BACP). BACP registered counsellors and therapists and UKCP (UK Council for Psychotherapy) registered therapists will be bound by the Code of Ethics and Practice demanded by these professional bodies. Counselling training is varied. Some training courses are very detailed and robust, others are more introductory. There are different methods of counselling, each with its own theoretical basis. The length of training for counsellors is varied according to how deeply and intensively trained they are. Some complete training after six months, others can train for two years. Some counselling training courses require the practitioner to undergo their own therapy, others don't.

There is now a field of training emerging called counselling psychology. Counselling psychologists' starting point is that no one philosophy of therapy should be adhered to and that a clinician should develop an eclectic way of working with the client, based on the client's needs. Counselling psychologists combine their understanding of psychology and, their ability to use assessments with talking therapy (counselling). Counsellors can work in a number of settings including schools, businesses, GP practices, in the NHS and at universities. A number of varied theoretical approaches can be adopted in counselling, including person centered therapy, developed by Carl Rogers, which focuses on empathic listening, unconditional regard for the client and reflecting back the feelings of the person who talks in the hope that an experience of having been understood (cognizance) enables them to make the necessary changes. As counsellors become more trained and experienced they absorb more complex theoretical thinking into their practice. On the whole counsellors tend to adapt their practice to the client' needs far more than adhering to a theoretical structure. Their training enables them to respond appropriately and in the "here and now" to what the client is expressing.

For more information, please contact:

British Association for Counselling and Psychotherapy (BACP):
    www.bacp.co.uk
UK Council for Psychotherapy (UKCP): www.ukcp.org.uk

Clinical psychologists

Clinical psychologists are individuals who train in psychology and go on to work in clinical settings. During their initial training they acquire an understanding of how the brain works, psychological research methodology and child development. Clinical psychologists aim to reduce psychological distress and enhance and promote psychological well-being. They work with people of all ages who experience mental or physical health problems. Most clinical psychologists work in health and social care settings including hospitals, health centres, community mental health teams, child and adolescent mental health services and social services. Some work as trainers, teachers and researchers in universities and some work in private practice. Clinical psychologists' interventions are usually short-term, because there is so much demand on their time within the National Health Service, although some are able to offer clients therapy for one or two years, once a week. The field is very competitive as there are few training opportunities available within the National Health Service.

Clinical psychologists are primarily concerned with the assessment and treatment of, and research into, psychological distress and well-being, and the psychological causes of physical illness. Most clinical psychologists work with a particular client group, the main categories being adults with mental health problems, children and families, people with learning disabilities, and older adults. Referrals come from a wide range of other professionals including hospital doctors, nurses, social workers, education professionals, health visitors, school health nurses, occupational therapists and physiotherapists. There is no requirement for clinical psychologists to have had their own therapy during training. This can sometimes be a disadvantage because the individual has not gone through the experience of being at the receiving end of therapeutic intervention. However, if they want to acquire really good skills in their field, most practitioners tend to have therapy themselves. Clinical psychologists sometimes use a range of psychological testing to better understand their client's personalities and needs. In England there is a shortage of training places for clinical psychologists as they can only train within the National Health Service and attached to a psychological department of a hospital. Clinical psychology training involves practical and academic learning. It is for this reason that very few training placements are provided. The field is therefore very competitive. Once a clinical psychologist has qualified they can specialize in specific areas of practice if they wish to do so. These could include forensics or clinical neuropsychology.

For more information, please contact:

The British Psychological Society: www.bps.org.uk

Educational psychologists

Educational psychologists initially apply for their training after having taught for a number of years as teachers. Educational psychologists are concerned with the application of psychological theory, research and techniques to helping children or young people who may have learning, behavioural, social or emotional problems or difficulties. Their work is usually conducted within an educational context. Some of the work is directly with individual children, which would involve an assessment of the child's presenting problem using different techniques, observation and discussion. Educational psychologists also provide in-service training for teachers and other professionals on issues such as behaviour management, truancy, stress management and assessment. Their work can also involve advising on educational provisions and policies and carrying out research. Educational psychologists are qualified to use a series of standard intelligence and personality tests. They do not have to have had therapy themselves.

For more information, please contact:

Association of Educational Psychologists (AEP): www.aep.org.uk

Cognitive behavioural psychologist or psychotherapists

Cognitive psychology is the psychological science that studies cognition, the mental processes that underlie behaviour, including thinking, deciding, reasoning and, to some extent, motivation and emotion. Cognitive psychologists tend to work either within the National Health Service or in clinics. Sometimes they can combine their work with behavioural therapy. Behavioural therapy assumes that the behaviour of an individual can be changed through the process of reward and punishment. Behavioural therapists are especially good with clients who suffer from phobias, because they can do a treatment called desensitization, which means gently and gradually exposing the client to the source of their phobia. For example, if the client is afraid of spiders, they would gently show the client a picture of spiders, get the client to relax and eventually increase it to a spider being in a jar and finally releasing the spider and allowing the client even to touch the spider. This process of desensitization can bring about behaviour modification. Behaviour therapists can help parents identify a behaviour in the child that they should ignore and help them see the behaviour in their child they should encourage. Through the process of responding to appropriate behaviour and not responding to inappropriate behaviour, it is thought that behaviour therapy can modify the way someone interacts with others in their environment. Cognitive behavioural therapists concentrate on the thinking which leads to behaviour and set about achieving changes in the beliefs and mindsets that underpin behaviour in the hope that the behaviour will change as a result. This approach is often referred to as CBT (Cognitive Behaviour Therapy). The therapist and the client will form a working alliance in the context of which the client's thinking is analyzed and through a series of homeworks the client is encouraged to change behaviours which are detrimental to their well-being. The change is thought to come about as a result of both addressing the thinking and practising new ways of behaviour. Sometimes the behaviour is addressed directly in the process of which there is hope that change will come about in the thinking, that is, a new way of behaving creates new thinking opportunities.

For more information, please contact:

British Association for Behavioural and Cognitive Psychotherapies
(BABCP): www.babcp.com

Psychotherapists

Psychotherapists, like counsellors, focus on talking to the client. However, unlike with counselling, trainee psychotherapists receive psychotherapy themselves as a required part of their training and preparation for practice. Psychotherapy training involves the individual training of the practitioner; usually this includes infant and child observation training and practical training in analyzing interactions with clients, as well as some academic study of various theories of psychotherapy. Psychotherapists approach the work according to the type of therapy they have trained in. These "talking treatments" include cognitive behavioural, psychoanalytic, psychodynamic, humanistic and integrative, Gestalt, experiential constructivist and existential therapies, and hypnopsychotherapy, amongst others. Psychotherapists are registered in the UK with the UK Council for Psychotherapy (UKCP) or the British Association for Counselling and Psychotherapy (BACP). The average psychotherapy training is usually four to five years and the trainee is required to have relevant experience in the field, for example having been a social worker or a teacher before joining the therapy school. Working with the client as an active participant, the psychotherapist offers the client the opportunity to address their thought processes, feelings and behaviour in order to understand inner conflicts and find new ways to deal with, and alleviate, their distress. Some psychotherapists use the transference relationship to understand how the client experiences object relations, others don't, preferring to work in the "here and now". Throughout their practice psychotherapists are encouraged to receive clinical supervision or engage in peer supervision. Not all clients are considered suitable for psychotherapy. A certain ability to process material on a mental level is thought to be a requirement. Some psychotherapists tend to work with the unconscious, others do not see it as essential. Psychotherapists work both privately and in a variety of professional settings.

For more information, please contact:

British Association for Counselling and Psychotherapy (BACP):
www.bacp.co.uk

Child psychotherapists

Child psychotherapists are intensively trained. Training prepares these therapists to treat children either individually, as part of and involving the family unit, and/or in a group setting. Child psychotherapy placements, which involve paid work as a trainee, are available from the National Health Service, but these are very limited. It is very expensive to train as a child psychotherapist as personal psychoanalysis is compulsory at least three times per week, and up until recently there were only three main schools of training: The Anna Freud Clinic, the Tavistock Clinic and the British Association of Psychotherapists (BAP) Clinic. More recently child psychotherapists with an arts background have also been registered, and they can be found at the Centre for Child Mental Health. Child psychotherapy training is detailed. In order to then work as an adult psychotherapist, most child psychotherapists would engage in a one-year conversion course. Conversely, it is not possible for an adult psychotherapist to convert to child psychotherapy training by doing a one year of training – they would usually be required to do the full training as child psychotherapy is thought to be a very specialized practice. Most child psychotherapists use play or talking in their therapy sessions. Some children are seen once a week, others may be seen twice or three times a week. In recognition of a significant shortage of child psychotherapists the profession has made an effort to widen its consultancy role so practitioners often give advice to schools, nurseries, health professionals and parents.

For more information, please contact:

British Association of Psychotherapists (BAP):
  www.bap-psychotherapy.org
Centre for Child Mental Health: www.childmentalhealthcentre.org
UK Council for Psychotherapy (UKCP): www.ukcp.org.uk

Art psychotherapists

Art therapy is the use of arts materials for self-expression and reflection in the presence of a trained art therapist. Art therapists may include drama therapists, dance movement therapists, art psychotherapists and body therapists. The overall aim of art therapy practitioners is to enable a client to effect change and growth on a personal level through the use of art psychotherapy in a safe and facilitating environment. Most art therapists train for an average of three years and they are required to undergo their own therapy. They must have competencies in the art field they have chosen and they must have their own art psychotherapy intervention during their training. Many are required to have relevant experience before they join the training. Art therapy differs from other psychological therapies in that it is a three-way process between the client, the therapist and the art form. Thus it offers the opportunity for expression and communication and can be particularly helpful to people who find it hard to express their thoughts and feelings verbally. Art therapists have a considerable understanding of art processes, underpinned by a sound knowledge of therapeutic practice, and work with both individuals and groups in a variety of residential and community-based settings, for example working with adults with mental health problems, people with learning disabilities, in child and family centres, in palliative care and in the prison service. The diversity of these areas of work is reflected in the number of special interest groups that have developed in affiliation with The British Association of Art Therapists (BAAT). Art therapists, drama and music therapists need to register with the Health Professions Council. The British Association of Art Therapists is the professional organization for art therapists in the United Kingdom and has its own Code of Ethics of Professional Practice.

For more information, please contact:

The British Association of Art Therapists (BAAT): www.baat.org

Play therapists

Play therapists work with children aged between three and eleven years of age and occasionally adolescents who suffer from a range of psychological difficulties and complex life experiences. The psychological difficulties which may be approached using play therapy include depression, anxiety, aggression, learning difficulties and ADHD. Play therapists work with children and often with those who have learning difficulties and cannot access language-based therapeutic intervention. Play therapists use play and art material in order to assist the client in communicating their concerns. Together they work through the various challenges the client faces. Play therapists' training duration varies depending on the school of training. They are usually required to have their own therapy and must have competencies in the field of play. They are registered with the British Association of Play Therapists (BAPT) and the Association for Play Therapy in the US. Play therapy can start as an introductory course, but as a qualification which is nationally recognized it needs to be acquired at postgraduate level. There is a requirement for the trainee to have undergone their own personal therapy and receive ongoing supervision. Play therapists can sometimes assist parents to reach children with communication disorders using play techniques. Some play therapy is used to develop pro-social capacities in children while other play therapy practitioners use the transference relationship to explore unconscious conflicts. In order to train as a play therapist practitioners need to have had relevant experience with children.

For more information, please contact:

The British Association of Play Therapists (BAPT): www.bapt.info

Psychoanalysts

Psychoanalysts are psychoanalytical therapists and are usually very detailed therapeutic practitioners. As part of their training they are often required to treat a minimum of two patients for psychoanalysis, five times a week, under clinical supervision. In addition to this they continue with their own personal analysis five times a week. As well as a robust theoretical and academic training, some psychoanalytic schools require trainees to do infant observation of a mother and baby. Trainees are required to have had relevant experience in the field and need approval from their personal analysts chosen by the training institute in order to commence formal training.

Psychoanalysis is an intense talking therapy which works primarily with the unconscious and the relationship between the client and the psychoanalyst. The theoretical emphasis is on working with the unconscious towards greater integration of the personality. Devised by Sigmund Freud, but developed continuously and radically since then, psychoanalysis extensively explores dreams and defence mechanisms. Psychoanalytic treatment is usually three to five times a week over a long period of time. It is intended to bring about fundamental changes in personality, enabling clients to function more appropriately and be at ease with themselves. Psychoanalysts use the interaction between themselves and the client to explore the client's object relations. They tend to focus a lot less on exploring problems and problem solving, unless these are expressive of the client's inner world. Psychoanalytic training is usually five years post-psychotherapy training and psychoanalysts have their own registered body. Those wanting to work with children have to train separately in the psychoanalysis of children and adolescents.

For more information, please contact:

British Psychoanalytic Council: www.bcp.org.uk
The British Psychoanalytical Society: www.psychoanalysis.org.uk

Family or group therapists

Family or group therapists work with individuals and groups using systems theories. The basis of their thinking is that the other family members impact the client's interactions and behaviour just as much as the client impacts the family system since they form part of the same group or system. Their goal is to make it easier for both group and individual to function together. Different training requirements are adhered to by different schools. Group analysts or psychotherapists are required to have undergone a mixture of personal, individual and group analysis. Family therapists tend to train and work as part of a team. The contribution of a group of clinicians is thought to illuminate the systemic structures underpinning family functioning.

For more information, please contact:

Association for Family Therapy (AFT): www.aft.org.uk

Substance Misuse:
A Tourist's Guide

Alcohol

Also known as bevy, booze, pop, etc.

Pure alcohol, or ethanol, is contained, in varying strengths, in all alcoholic drinks, depending on the other ingredients and the quantity of ethanol used. The strength of alcoholic drinks is given as a percentage of volume – the higher the volume, the stronger the drink. Pure alcohol is poisonous.

Alcohol is absorbed into the bloodstream and the amount of alcohol present in all parts of the body is known as blood alcohol concentration (BAC). BAC is determined by a variety of factors, including body weight, type and quantity of alcohol and whether or not food has been consumed – alcohol is absorbed more slowly into the bloodstream if it is drunk with or after a meal. One "unit" of alcohol is equivalent to half a pint of beer, a glass of wine or a single measure of spirits, and it take about an hour for the liver to process and remove one unit of alcohol from the body. Even in small amounts, alcohol can help people relax, lose their inhibitions and become animated. When larger amounts of alcohol are consumed, these effects are amplified and can lead to people becoming aggressive, loud and possibly violent.

Doctors say that drinking alcohol in moderation can help prevent coronary heart disease; the current recommended limit on alcohol intake is two to three units per day for women and three to four units per day for men. Consuming more than six units in six hours is classified as "binge" drinking.

Alcohol consumed in large quantities negatively affects coordination, judgement and mood. In extreme cases it can lead to alcohol poisoning, which can be fatal. In the UK, over a thousand people under the age of fifteen are admitted to hospital each year and given emergency treatment for alcohol poisoning, according to the National Drugs Helpline.

Amphetamines

Also known as amph, base, billy, buzz, crank, crystal, ice, meth, rocks, speed, sulphate, uppers, white, whiz, yabba

In the 1930s, amphetamine was introduced as a new medication against a stuffy nose, and during the Second World War it was given to soldiers to increase alertness. In the 1950s and 1960s it began to be used to treat depression and weight control. Today it is a class B drug that is sniffed, smoked and taken intravenously and orally. It is sold in the form of tablets, capsules, powder, liquid and crystals. As stimulants to the central nervous system, amphetamines cause a feeling of well-being and energy, and larger doses lead to restlessness, feelings of superiority and strength. Many users display aggressive or hostile behaviour. The physiological effects of amphetamines include lack of appetite, increased heart rate and blood pressure and dilated pupils, with larger doses causing sweating, headaches, reduced vision and faintness. Amphetamine poisoning manifests itself in disturbed heartbeat, cramps and a loss of coordination. Regular use of amphetamines can lead to malnourishment and a weakened immune system, as well as unpredictable and violent behaviour resulting from delusions of persecution – so-called amphetamine psychosis has symptoms similar to paranoid schizophrenia. Long-term use can cause psychological dependency and tolerance increases with constant use so higher doses are taken to achieve the same effect. Amphetamines increase the likelihood of stroke and deaths following amphetamine use are usually triggered by cerebral haemorrhage, stroke and high fever.

Cannabis

Also known as bhang, black, blast, blow, blunts, bob hope, buds, bush, diesel, dope, draw, ganja, gold, grass, hash, hashish, hemp, herb, honey, marijuana, mary jane, northern lights, oil, pot, puff, resin, sensi, sensemilla, shit, skunk, smoke, soap, spliff, wacky backy, weed and zero

Cannabis is a natural substance derived from the Cannabis sativa plant, which is easily cultivated and found wild in most parts of the world. Cannabis is available in the form of leaves, stalks and seeds – "grass", solid dark lumps of resin, or as sticky oil. It is smoked with tobacco in a "spliff" or "joint" or on its own in a pipe or "bong", and it can be an ingredient in a cake, cookie or tea, when its effects are often stronger and less predictable. Some forms, for example "skunk", are very strong and can cause a hallucinogenic reaction. Cannabis was used as a herbal medicine by the Chinese in the first century AD and it is being rediscovered for the relief of pain in the advanced stages of cancer, AIDS and other serious illnesses. Cannabis can make the user relax and is often seen by users as a drug that doesn't unduly effect their judgement and abilities. Its mild but noticeable physiological effects are increased pulse rate, decreased blood pressure, bloodshot eyes, a dry mouth and increased appetite ("the munchies"). It also intensifies the perception of colours, tastes and music, and can produce increased sociability, talkativeness and hilarity, or introspection. Prolonged use or stronger varieties may lead to tiredness and lack of energy. As with tobacco, smoking cannabis can lead to lung and other cancers as well as other smoking-related diseases. Cannabis use affects short-term memory, levels of concentration and coordination, which makes this drug as dangerous as alcohol in its effects on the ability to drive a car, ride a bike or operate machinery. Long-term users may experience paranoia and anxiety, depression and apathy, and in people with a family history of schizophrenia cannabis has been associated with triggering the condition.

Cocaine

Also known as Bolivian, C, Charlie, coke, dust, gold dust, marching powder, Percy, snow, white, white lady, bugle

Cocaine is an extract of coca plant leaves and is a very strong stimulant. It was a common anaesthetic and popular "tonic" in the early twentieth century, before the 1920 Dangerous Drugs Act banned its use. Today it is a class A drug usually sold in powder form that is snorted up the nose, absorbed through the gums, or dissolved and injected by users. It gives the user a sense of well-being, confidence and alertness but produces a craving for more when the hit wears off. The physiological effects of the drug include an increase in body temperature, heart rate and blood pressure as well as dilated pupils, lasting for about half an hour, followed by a comedown associated with depression and tiredness that can last for a couple of days. The severity of the comedown means users may take more and more cocaine to delay it, which often results a psychological dependence that can costs thousands of pounds a year. Frequent snorting of cocaine can damage the septum and causes nosebleeds and ulcers. Long-term use can lead to panic attacks, paranoia, depression and, in extreme cases, cocaine psychosis (similar to schizophrenia). Chest pain, heart problems, convulsions can occur with heavy use. If taken in large enough doses, cocaine can be fatal.

Crack

Also known as base, flake, freebase, gravel, , nuggets, pebbles, rocks, Roxanne, stones, wash

Crack is a highly addictive drug. It comes in small, irregular lumps that are smoked and produce an effect similar to cocaine but far more powerful – the hit is very short-lived, very intense and makes the user feel very euphoric, strong and energetic. The comedown is equally extreme and leaves users fatigued and weak. Dependent users become paranoid and antagonistic, and overdose of crack can lead to respiratory and heart failure, coma and death.

Heroin

Also known as brown, china white, dragon, gear, H, Harry, horse, jack, junk, shit, skag, smack

Heroin is an opiate made from morphine extracted from the latex in the seeds of the opium poppy. Other opiates include diamorphine and methadone. Heroin was used as a painkiller in the nineteenth century until doctors realized that it was highly addictive. Today it is a class A drug, usually sold as a brownish-white powder of variable purity. The drug is often "cut" with other substances, such as chalk, flour, talcum powder and caffeine, and these impurities mean it is often difficult to gauge its strength, which increases the risk of overdose. Heroin is smoked, snorted, or dissolved and injected and takes effect within just a few seconds. Users have an instant feeling of well-being and feel relaxed and drowsy when taking larger doses. The physiological effects of taking heroin are blurred vision, constricted pupils, sweating, slow breathing, nausea and vomiting. Heroin use also impairs concentration, suppresses pain and can induce anxiety. Both physically and psychologically, heroin is very addictive, and users are compelled to take larger and larger doses just to feel normal. Large doses can lead to stupor and coma, and overdoses are often fatal. Heroin is generally injected, and using unclean or shared needles poses serious risks of infection from HIV, hepatitis and other diseases. Withdrawal effects can be dramatic – initially the user suffers aches, hot and cold sweats, sneezing and spasms that peak after about three days and recede after about ten days, although fatigue and weakness may be experienced for several months afterwards. Methadone, a synthetic opiate, is prescribed to treat heroin addiction, but it is as addictive as heroin and has to be strictly controlled for those wanting to kick the habit.

LSD (lysergic acid diethylamide) and other hallucinogenics

Also known as acid, blotter, cheer, dots, drop, flash, hawk, L, lightening flash, liquid acid, Lucy, magics, micro-dot, paper mushrooms, rainbows, shrooms, smilies, stars, tab, trips, trippers, windows

There are a wide range of synthetic hallucinogenics, such as LSD and phencyclidine (PCP), and natural hallucinogenics, such as pscilosybin, mescalin. LSD has a dramatic effect even in small doses and is the strongest known hallucinogenic. In its pure form it is a white, odourless, water-soluble powder but it is usually sold in the form of "tabs" – small, colourful pieces of paper that are taken orally – though it can also be taken as a liquid absorbed in sugar cubes, paper etc. or as a capsule or tablet. LSD causes powerful hallucinations – users may feel as one with the universe and outside their own bodies or have synaesthetic experiences – "seeing music" or "hearing colours". Some users take LSD in the hope that they have a mystic, religious or cosmic experience. The psychological effects of hallucinogenics are very varied – depending on the individual, experiences can be ecstatic or horrifying (or change from one to the other in one "trip") and are entirely unpredictable and unrelated to previous hallucinogenic experiences. Effects usually last between two to twelve hours but may last up to two days. The physiological effects are increased blood pressure and heartbeat and dilated pupils, while sensory, time and self perception are dramatically altered. "Bad trips" can cause nausea, depression, anxiety, hallucinations and panic attacks, as well as "flashbacks" – spontaneous trips without having taken the drug that can occur months or years after the last dose. Hallucinogenics are not generally addictive.

Glue and other solvents

Also known as amyl, can, cog, gas, glue, huff, poppers and sniff

Ether and gases were inhaled from the nineteenth century, but sniffing glues and nail varnish remover became widespread in the 1960s. "Sniffing" is the smelling and inhaling of solvents that produces effects similar to those of taking drugs. Everyday household products such as cleaning products, glues, nail varnish remover and lighter fuel are commonly used for sniffing. Solvents are quickly absorbed into the blood stream and produce euphoria, confusion and hallucinations as well as unpredictable behaviour. They also cause slow reflexes, light sensitivity, coordination difficulties, nausea and respiratory problems. The effects of sniffing can last up to twelve hours but the "hangover" and headache caused by the fumes can persist several days.

Rapid and continuous sniffing in a short period of time may lead to unconsciousness and stroke. Long-term use can result in physiological effects such as nosebleeds, bloodshot eyes, lung, kidney and liver damage and weight loss; some solvents can lead to brain failure. Other symptoms include mental problems and depression, violence, paranoia and fatigue.